Confessions
Of A
Car Dealer

Buyer's Guide
To Your Best Car Deal

LEE

DEDICATION

This book is dedicated to Larry D.; who suggested I get into this business in the
first place. With no prior experience, I told him I had never even sold a car, and
his answer to me was, "I don't want you to sell cars, I want you for a closer!"
When I asked what a closer was, he said, "I'll teach you everything you need to
know." So I began my retail automobile career with Larry "loading my lips" with
what to say, including the body language to use every time, and *I hit the ground
running*, and never looked back. I learned enough to *run with the big dogs*, and in six
months I bought my first car dealership.

Thanks Larry.

CONTENTS

INTRODUCTION

"A man could be killed for this!" My friend that spoke these words may be correct, but this book will only expose the dishonest practices used by dealers who deserve no quarter.

As I sit on my lanai, awaiting what this year's hurricane season will bring, I wonder about the hurricane this book might create by blowing the roof off the retail car business!

I thought long and hard before finally exposing these dirty tricks, lies, con games and outright dishonest practices; and concluded that I must do so, maybe it's my way to set things right.

I was warned against bringing such heat on the industry that had made me so much money, but I realize that these schemes do so much irreparable harm that it must all end!

The flagrant abuse of the American car buyer has put a damper on America's most unique pastime — buying cars!

This book will put you on even ground with the car dealer!

These secrets have never before been put in writing, because they cannot be researched! They are only taught to successive generations of select management, and then, only verbally. Nothing is written down, because of the liability!

The reader will be given an extensive overview of the inner workings of the entire purchasing experience in order to understand all of the pitfalls and traps that await the unsuspecting car buyer.

Then, in easy to understand instructions, you will learn how to find out what the dealer paid for his car, what your trade in is worth in actual cash money, and how to find your lowest available interest rate.

You will learn how to calculate your own payments within eight seconds, and the easy and hassle-free way to negotiate your best deal!

No more long sessions of *haggling* and *brain damage*! Just a quick, easy and friendly car buying experience.

There are pages of warnings, and key words and phrases to watch out for, and the very big *black hole* that you must learn about; the dealer's extra profit centers that pay him *all the money*!

The hidden world of finance, leasing, and the *optional* profit makers. Learn the truth about extended warranties, credit insurance, and the gadgets and gimmicks that earn fortunes for the dealer, and have little or no value whatsoever to the purchaser!

The author will carefully instruct you as to what to watch for, the con games that go on before and after your purchase, and how to look for traps once you drive off the lot!

Your 10th car free? This book will prepare the reader to save enough money on each future negotiation that the tenth transaction should be paid for by the accumulated savings on the first nine!

Before we enter the dark world of the car deal, I would like to introduce the players:

> *Salesperson* — No matter what title they are given, their job is to help you select a vehicle you like. Then they need to explain all of the features and benefits of the selected vehicle, and make you fall in love with it! They will then ask you, "If the figures are agreeable, will you buy it and drive it home now?" If you say, "No," they will *turn* you to another salesperson who will repeat the procedure. If you agree to buy it, they will begin writing your offer.

Closer — In dealerships where the salesperson does not participate in the final negotiations, this is the person whom you will negotiate the entire transaction with. The closer may be called by numerous titles; sales manager, assistant manager, floor manager, team leader, whatever innocuous title works, but the closer's job, in addition to training sales teams, is to negotiate! Period! This is the person who is the most talented negotiator, and the structure is a simple one; run every customer through your most talented closer and they will make *all the money*. This way the salesperson only has to concentrate on selecting a vehicle and getting a commitment to buy, and the closer only trains them and closes their deals.

Desk or *Sales manager* — Desk seems to be a slang term that has become so much a part of our conversation that it even slips out in front of customers. It is derived by the sharing of responsibilities among management, and means whoever is acting sales manager, as in, "Who's on the desk?" Meaning, who is running the sales office at the time. There may be many desk managers in a dealership that take turns.

Many times, as customers often suspect; there is no one in the office at all! The closer goes into the sales office, calculates the new figures, writes the numbers on the *worksheet* with a big marker and *desks* himself. Then he takes the offer back to the customer and says, "This is what my boss will do." Each offer brought before a customer is referred to as a *pencil*. When we refer to the last pencil, it means our last offer to the buyer. Common language among us is, "How many pencils did it take to shut 'em?" This means, "How many passes did it take (pencils) in order to close (shut) the sale?"

This is why closers are often referred to as *shutters*. Therefore, in dealerships that employ closers to negotiate all transactions, we refer to them as a *system house*. A system house has liners (salespeople) and closers (sales managers). As I mentioned, the process of the system is that every customer is run through the dealer's most talented people.

The closers and desk managers in these operations are *highly compensated*, so what may appear to be a *Columbo* type of stumbling manager to you, may be earning huge dollars for the performance!

Now that we understand the players and some of their terminology, let's learn how to survive in this pool of sharks and not get eaten!

CHAPTER 1
FIRST, LET'S LOOK AT WHAT YOU'RE UP AGAINST

Wouldn't it be nice if you could walk into an automobile dealership and just get straight and honest answers?

Well, it won't happen, and even if it did, would you believe them? That's exactly why it won't happen!

Buying cars, trucks and R.V.s has always involved negotiating, and that's the reason that dealers have salespeople rather than assistant buyers or clerks.

These people are paid a commission based on the profit they make on a sale. The more you pay, the more they earn!

So, in order to avoid paying too much profit, the buyer must negotiate.

Consider this book as a *consumer's guide* to negotiating strategies. A crash course in how not to get *taken*; in easy to understand terms.

Many people enter this arena with no preparation at all. They just feel that if they are offensive enough, and negotiate hard enough that they will win.

This is the part that is not only distasteful to the womenfolk, but also unnecessary, and stressful for everyone involved! I'll teach you how to do it the easy way and without the mental frustration.

We will also discuss self-defense for the female buyer. Since women either make or directly influence and control the majority of all automobile purchases, they need this information even more than their male counterparts! Did you think that car people were unaware of this? Way ahead of you!

A woman who shops for a vehicle will generally be a lot more cautious in her decision making than a man. Women are also much more obvious in their contempt for the negotiating process. She can't understand why she has to perform in the same *dog and pony show* that men seem to relish. The lady would just like to see the lowest price at which she may purchase the vehicle she has chosen. Then, she would like to see the value of her trade-in, what her monthly cost will be, and at what interest rate. Then she could make her comparison with other dealerships, which is the way she makes other purchases.

It just isn't that easy, is it? A male dominated car business, and a female dominated buying public, just don't blend all that easy. Ever try to get all of that information right up front at a car dealership? You can't, right? Of course not, and once I give you the reasons, it will make sense.

This book will give the reader the psychology that the dealer employs against the unmarried female, who out of self-preservation, asks *Mr. Macho* to accompany her to the dealership and how she generally ends up paying more profit due to his ego!

Lest you think the car business is still locked in the past, they are way ahead of you! For my entire career, I taught my salespeople to spend the majority of their presentation directed to the wife, regardless of who the vehicle was for. I had a sign in the sales office entitled "Lee's Rule of 95." It stated, "In 95% of all cases, the wife will make the buying decision, and in the other 5% she *allows* her husband to do it!" So you see, we are aware of who controls the purchase!

So why does the in-control female take the easily-controlled male along with her to buy a car? Maybe it's from a slight *Neanderthal* thinking process? Just because she doesn't like the process, she thinks she can't participate in it? It is no longer sensible that a woman should continue in such a subservient role when it comes to car buying when males have already proven that they are not any good at it. *Look at it like the jungle, and let the lioness make the kill, and her man can sit on his ass and roar!*

No ladies, that means that no longer is it fair, or even proper, for you to sit in your car and make your poor husband run back and forth between you and the dealer doing the negotiating! Playing *ostrich* may have worked in the Victorian Era, but please grow up and exercise your rightful place at the bargaining table and leave your *sensibilities* at home! Car dealers no longer buy your thin-skinned attitude and your husband needs your strength.

A man or woman who comes in to a dealership without the solid authority to make a decision is referred to as a *one-legger*. One-leggers seldom are given much more than courtesy and general information. Trade-ins are not appraised ("The appraiser is out," etc.), payments are not accurately calculated, and prices are only discussed in generalities and estimates.

Here the salesperson walks a *thin line*. They must be courteous and polite enough to give the customer enough information so they will return with their partner. They will not get too specific however, or quote *bottom line* figures, or they set themselves up for comparison shopping.

So you ask, why don't they just give their *best deal* and let a person compare? This would be the best for the consumer, but in order for a dealer to earn their business, he would have to have the lowest price and the highest trade allowance. To do this on a consistent basis, the dealer would have to also accept the lowest profit margin and he would not survive!

Accompany this low profit margin with the inevitable repair costs with trade-ins that have problems that were *undisclosed* from the people who traded them in, and you have a recipe for failure.

The car business has a saying that may surprise some of you, "Buyers are liars!" So you see, the consumer also has a bad reputation when it comes to honest dealing.

There is another big reason for why you cannot easily get a *best price* from a dealer. Say for example, that you come to me with a request for a bottom line number, and I give it to you with the promise to buy from me if you can't beat it. You now go shopping, and maybe you are in a large metropolitan area, and you check six other dealers, all with the same car as I have. Let's say that you get to the last dealer who is maybe closer to your home than I am, because you began your search at my store because it was the furthest away. Now let's say that the other dealer starts out by negotiating hard with you, and after a long *haggling* session he meets my price.

Everything being exactly equal, are you still going to honor your word to me? Remember, I'm the guy that gave you the best deal right up front, and without hassle. The other guy really worked hard and put you through a lot of negotiating to meet my deal! I'll ask you again, "Will you come back to me?" I hope you didn't answer yes, because I don't believe you for a minute! You will not come back me, because the general public does not believe that lying to a car dealer is wrong. The car dealer is the *bad guy*, and lying to him is perfectly acceptable!

This is why I can truthfully say that over my career, I have been lied to and cheated by every member of every profession, from politicians, law enforcement, the clergy, and that means every denomination there is, and I cannot think of any group or occupation that hasn't tried to slip me a bad transmission, weak engine, massive unseen damage, or a host of problems that didn't even surface until my service department tried to prepare a vehicle for resale. So you see, car people don't trust you anymore than you trust them!

Let's forget about trust from here on out, and just concentrate on what we need to do in order to negotiate our best deal! In our previous scenario, if you would feel bad for breaking your word by not returning to the original dealer, all you need to do is tell the other guy to give you one dollar more discount, and that way you can save face, and you will not have broken your word.

Now, let's go back to another gender comparison. Women have always hated being treated like second-class citizens when shopping for a car without their spouse; feeling it to be discourteous and rude when they couldn't come away with anything other than generalities. Now, a man, on the other hand, you can pretty much tell to go home and get his wife and then we'll negotiate a good deal, and he naturally accepts it and will return with her as instructed. Because of these differences in how the sexes react to being fed B.S., we handle the women more professionally, spend more time on the test drive, and make them feel better about how they are treated. They still get very little solid information however.

By learning the information in this book, you may change your standard of living! This may seem like a big boast, but think about this; if you had another one to five hundred dollars a month in spendable income, would your standard of living be different?

I'll show you how to negotiate well enough to change your life, but you must do your part. You can't be too fragile or uppity to negotiate! You cannot feel insulted because a car dealer wants to make a lot of money. That's his job! That's how he survives. I'll teach you how to courteously and professionally negotiate a terrific deal. Read on, and let's have some fun in buying!

LEE

CHAPTER 2
PROPER SELECTION IS A MUST – AND NO, YOU CAN'T RETURN IT

I cannot emphasize strongly enough to select the right vehicle! You would find it staggering the number of customers I had each month who had made the wrong decision when they purchased their present vehicle and wanted to get out of it in less than a year. If I personally saw that many, think of how many thousands upon thousands of people in this country are in the same position.

Now it may not seem to be that big a deal, but let me assure you that if you aren't very careful when you select your next vehicle, it can have devastating consequences. Consider this; you purchase a vehicle, and all things considered, let's say the dealer only makes a profit of a thousand dollars. If you traded your old vehicle in, the dealer would stock it in his books at less than its' wholesale value, so that after all reconditioning and detailing he could still own it for somewhat below its *true* wholesale value. This means that you gave up your trade-in for one to two thousand dollars below its' wholesale value, and several thousand dollars less than you could have received for it had you taken the time to sell it retail through the newspaper, online, or other means.

Also, if you had a negative equity in your trade-in, which a huge percentage of people do, you just carried additional negative forward because you *cheap sold* your trade. Now you find out you don't like the vehicle you just bought! If you just lost several thousand dollars on the previous transaction, where do you think you're going to be value-wise now? What will likely happen now is that you will either have to suffer with a vehicle you don't like, or get ready for an even worse beating when you trade it again. You were buried before, now you're even buried deeper, and to sell your vehicle, you must compete with the dealer who can sell someone a brand new one for way less than you owe on your *slightly-used* trade.

Automobile dealers are in the business to make money. No matter how much you think they care about you and your needs, see how their attitude changes when you try to explain how you just made a terrible mistake by driving home with your new car the day before, and all you request is they let you out of the deal (unwind) and trade back. Your pleas will fall on deaf ears. Car dealers don't trade back! Once you drive it across the curb, it's yours. You own it, period!

You will get no sympathy from your dealer or salesperson. Look at it from their standpoint, whatever you do for a living, consider this; payday comes and you receive your check. The next day your boss comes in and asks you for some of it back, saying the company's profit picture had changed, and we need you to help us out. Get the picture? How would you feel then? That's what would happen if the dealer undid the transaction.

When you drive away, the salesperson and managers mentally make their bank deposit for the commission they just earned. They may call home and tell their spouse they just earned the rent, the new TV, the new flooring, etc. Now you come in after they've mentally spent the money and ask for it back. Are you nuts? What do you think they're going to say? Oh sure Mr. Customer, I like you so much that I will call my wife right now and tell her that I'm going to sacrifice her new tile floor to help out my nice customer that she's never met. Fat chance!

Do you begin to understand that maybe even though you developed a fondness for your salesperson and you both genuinely like each other, that maybe that's not enough? How would you react if your dealer phoned you, or better still, came to your home the next day and demanded more money for the vehicle you just purchased, saying he realized that he had made a terrible mistake on the price? Maybe you can begin to understand why all purchases are final! *No, you do not* have 72 hours to rescind the deal, unless you have an agreement in writing allowing you a rescission period, which you won't have.

People buy cars largely on an emotional level. Many falsely believe that they have this 72 hour *cooling off period,* and the salespeople let them go right along believing it! Why not? It sure makes their sale go easier. Once you drive it over the curb however, it's all yours!

As I mentioned previously, the number of people who regret their car buying decisions in the first year of ownership is tremendous! Don't join these statistics! Plan, research, and examine all possible scenarios before you buy a vehicle. If you don't, and if you make just a couple of wrong decisions, you could just jeopardize your chance of buying a home, or other far reaching consequences that could have a tremendously negative impact on your future!

Don't buy on impulse! People seldom buy newer vehicles because they need them. People buy cars for what cars do for their sense of well-being. We reward ourselves for achievements, or oftentimes for the fact that we have not achieved, so we boost our egos with a new automobile. No matter what you live in or how you live, when your fellow employees see you, they see what you wear and what you drive. Wherever you go, people accept you at face value and what better acceptance can you get than the thumbs up attitude that surrounds your purchase of a new car.

Whether it's a brand new or a used car, when I say new, it is the same. It's new to you, your friends, coworkers, etc. That's why so many people will go to a dealership to buy a different car than what they have if for no other reason than to be noticed by others.

A person who is in the rut of a steady job with steady pay, and no ups, downs or anything else different happening in his life, will create his own rewards and accolades by the purchase of a new car.

I'll discuss financing in another chapter, but let me say now, it will influence a foolish rationale when it comes to making a buying decision. I'll show you how to get more car for your money. How to make the same payment work on the car you really want rather than settle for a lesser model that you'll feel compelled to trade too soon.

An automobile is not an investment. It is a necessary expense in our society, but also can be a horrific waste of money if you trade too often. Put your money into a home instead.

If, when you go to look at cars, it doesn't turn out like you planned, leave! Go home, re-group and re-think your situation. You don't have to buy the first time out. Also, make sure that if you intend to only make a particular car work for three years, don't finance it for a term longer than three years if you can help it.

People are constantly financing for longer and longer terms in order to keep payments low, but then trading in short terms. What happens to any possibility of equity when you trade like that? There is none, of course. That's why the majority of trade-ins are worth less than what's owed on them.

So you finance a car for six years and trade it in three, then finance the next car for six years and trade it in three and so on. What happens to all that negative equity? It's carried over to each successive new purchase, and unless you're putting large down payments each time, you will eventually get to the point where a lender will refuse to grant the amount needed to finance another purchase.

By the time many people hit this point, it's oftentimes gone far enough to cause serious problems. With a good credit history, lenders will be very likely to carry this negative equity over to the new loan without question, and they will often do this time and time again, because they are relying on the credit worthiness of the individual rather than on the value of any collateral. So by the time a person finally has reached the limit of common sense in banking, they could well owe over twice the value of their car. Now if this time comes at a critical juncture in ones' life, when they really need to trade, they may just be in bad trouble. It can be something as simple as this that can trigger repercussions that can ruin a persons' future. If this sounds melodramatic, well, I see it every single week.

Bad buying decisions on cars can rob you of any chance to recover down the road. At the very least, a bankruptcy or repossession, or charged off loan will stay on your credit report for *ten* years. So whatever else you do, exercise extreme caution in the vehicle you decide to buy. The decision you make today can and will affect you for many, many years to come.

No matter what the car companies claim, vehicles depreciate! Rapidly! Trucks and Sport Utilities hold values better, but don't get overconfident because of the hype from your boss who just bought the newest luxury car on the market, or the salesperson who tells you how great you'll do when you trade. The only track record ever established on an automobiles' future value is down!

Also, don't be fooled when certain vehicles are scarce and the salesperson shows you the asking price on a used one at a price almost as high as the new one. This doesn't necessarily mean that the value is holding, it may just mean one hell of a high markup on the used car! Whatever seems so scarce and desirable today, will certainly be made in greater numbers and have droves of similar competing models right around the corner. No manufacturer ever makes a product so desirable that someone else won't produce a competitor, and the increased price you paid will plummet lower for the next guy.

If you finance your vehicle for five years, then make sure you can restrain yourself from trading before that time. Most, and I do mean most people that plan to drive a car for five years, end up financing or leasing for five, six, or seven years and trading in three -- Don't get caught up in it.

Look at your car buying history; How often have you traded in the past? Did you buy your last vehicle with the idea that you would keep it for many years? Then you discovered that you didn't really like it like you thought you would? Your needs changed, you saw another car you just had to have. If you're like most buyers, this is what almost always happens!

Make your buying decision with discipline. Tell yourself that whatever happens, you will live with this decision! You will hear me repeat this often, because you never should forget to not act impulsively! There is a saying in the car business, "Impulse buyers are God's gift to the car dealer!"

CHAPTER 3
LOOK BEFORE YOU LEAP

You see how important it is to make the right choice the first time. If you buy the wrong vehicle, you will soon be trading it off and cost yourself thousands!

To properly go about your search you first need to prepare a plan and then stick to it! Above all else, do not make a buying decision until you have completed your plan.

Some buyers shop themselves to death and never seem ready to make a decision. I do not suggest a laborious search involving months of preparation, but before we enter the marketplace there are a few important factors that we need to be aware of.

Most importantly, we must make sure that whatever we buy will fit into our budget. The budget you set must allow for not only the monthly payment, but also insurance, fuel consumption, maintenance and also the length of time we intend to keep it.

Let's say you have decided to buy a new passenger car and plan to keep it for three years. Then you go about budgeting for the payment and find the only way you can keep the payment to what you can afford is to finance it for six years. If this is the only way you can afford to purchase what you want, then maybe you can't afford to buy it right now, but if no other way to keep from buying it, then plan to own it for six years if you can, and common sense says you must!. Now be careful, because this is a long commitment, and I'd bet money you'll never honor it.

The unseen factor in deciding your budget for your purchase is what position you will be in when you are again ready to upgrade in three years. Remember, you financed it for six years. Unless you're exceptionally lucky, you won't have any equity in the car when it's time to trade. No, most likely you will have a *negative equity;* that is simply that you will owe more on it than it's worth.

So now in order to trade, you must either fork over the difference in cash, or carry this negative amount forward to your next vehicle. If you have the credit worthiness to enable you to accomplish this, your new payment will not only be higher than it should, but also, now you are still paying that negative amount that you carried forward for a new loan term, and paying extra interest on it. Assuming that you still need six year financing in order to keep your payment within budget; then you are financing the negative balance based on a six year pay-out. Since you already paid on the previous vehicle for three years, you're now carrying some of the money for nine years!

If you follow this same pattern, and again trade in three years, you now will likely be in the situation whereby you now have negative equity to carry forward on two cars! The remaining balance from the first, and of course, the greater negative balance on the second.

As you can plainly see, eventually, unless you change your pattern of thinking, you will get in deeper and deeper until either you will be forced to stop trading, or you will expand your vehicle budget beyond the reasonable limit. This is where your debt to income ratio may prevent you from purchasing a home! Worse yet, you may end up in a financial crisis. Start being late on your car payment a few times and soon you won't be able to obtain further credit for anything!

Don't let this happen! Determine either to shorten your loan term to match your projected ownership term, which will raise your monthly payment. Or, plan to live with your purchase for a longer time.

If you carefully select your car to meet future needs as well as present wants, you can stretch your term of ownership longer. Use the Financing chapter to find your payment and then see for what term and what amount of loan you will be able to fit into your budget.

There are so many consumer product guides on the market today that you should be able to do almost endless research on repair records, value retention and serviceability of any product. While you're researching, of course the main part of making a proper decision is to physically examine the vehicle. So we must make the dreaded trip to the car dealership. Go with the proper attitude. Don't expect a car salesperson to not try to sell you something. They work on commission, not salary, although some dealers advertise that their sales people are *salaried;* it's not true. There has to be an incentive to make larger profits, or a dealer could not survive. If they insist on that story, call their bluff. They are lying, and tell them to stop! Also, keep in mind that they make nothing for helping you do your research. So if you desire to have good service and a test drive, you *do not* tell this salesperson that you are first doing research and have no intention of buying on the spot.

Tell them that and you'll get politeness, courtesy and a very small amount of their time. Why? Because most car buyers will take whatever time the salesperson has to give and then have no loyalty to that person when it comes time to buy, and the salespeople are well aware of this. At least, when you are ready, and someone has spent time with you, remember they do get paid only when they make a sale, so go back to the same person, it's only courteous.

Back to the game. Remember you are there to look at, smell, feel, drive and compare. Nothing else. Make note of equipment, manufacturer's suggested list price on new vehicles, asking price on used vehicles, but don't worry too much about anything else at this time. Your objective at this point is *only* to select the vehicle. *Don't* bother to ask what your trade is worth because you won't get factual information anyway. Don't bother to even enter into negotiations because you're not prepared! Look at the vehicles in your predetermined price range as derived from reading the Finance chapter in this book. Make certain that you stick to your plan. Don't be swayed by supposed sales and other gimmicks that we in the business will use to try to motivate you to stop shopping and buy now. Look at every product that you intended to when you started out.

Now, let's say you started out to look at small pickup trucks. You're on the lot and suddenly see a sport utility rig that really changes your thinking. You see that you can carry more passengers and also use it to haul cargo with the seats folded down. Should you go ahead and buy it? No! Your plan *must be redone*! Now you must research the market on sport utilities or you could well make that impulsive, costly decision that you'll be sorry about the next day when it's too late!

So things change. Needs, wants, desires can change easily once you go car shopping. It is a very wise decision to just drive around looking at what is available before you even start paper research. Whenever your plan changes, you need to rework your budget. Then, working from the Finance chapter, work backwards and see what price range you can afford to shop in.

Sound like a lot of work? It should be. Statistics show that 43% of automobile purchasers express a major concern that they have either purchased the wrong vehicle, or could have made a better deal had they waited. That's 43%; almost half of all buyers! And that's within twenty-four hours after driving home with their purchase! You guessed right if you're thinking, *no right to rescind*. If the facts were known, the percentage who could have actually made a better deal is far greater than that.

The reason that people have regrets is because most are *impulse buyers*; the *lifeblood of the car business*. An impulse buyer is the one who gets caught up in the excitement of a new vehicle and just throws caution to the wind. My very favorite type of buyer!

To do proper research, there are hosts of publications such as Consumer Reports as an initial source of starting. When you see the ratings, take time to study the repair and breakdown records. Quality on vehicles like Lexus, Toyota, Honda and Acura is generally rated very high, but they also are prone to slip. Now that the domestics received a wake-up call, maybe they'll be worth another shot. I know they are better than they ever were. They would have to be!

When searching for one of these higher rated vehicles on the used car market, you will likely pay more than you would pay for a competitor's vehicle that cost the same price when new. Don't be fooled into paying too much though, and make certain that you see maintenance records whenever possible, and have it independently checked regardless.

Although these are just a few vehicles that rate very high in Consumer Reports, they also require a lot of ongoing maintenance to keep them functioning properly. You'd think after all of the years that motor vehicles have been manufactured that they would have *bullet-proof* transmissions, but that's not the case. It is not unusual for some vehicles to have a record of transmission failure over several consecutive years. If you buy a vehicle that has a good reputation by consumer's guides and reports, your odds are just better, but not necessarily worth all that much more money.

Many less expensive vehicles tout exceptionally long term factory warranties. Read that warranty carefully to see what items are covered and for how long. Many warranties cover electrical items for only the first twelve months and then different items are covered for longer, etc. Some warranties are only good for the original owner, and don't offer coverage for the second buyer, even if still within the warranty period. This will affect your value when you trade or sell.

So, researching will take time. How much time will be determined by the importance of the purchase to you. I will say that a large majority of buyers don't spend nearly enough time researching before they make this important a buying decision!

Maybe buying a make with a better track record will cost too much more than its' less well made and lower priced competitor to be able to fit it in your budget. Do keep in mind however, that the costs of vehicle breakdown, even though covered by warranties, are still costly in terms of loss of work and substitute vehicle costs. No, most warranties do not supply you with a loaner car when your car is in for warranty work. Maybe a lesser equipped model of a more highly rated vehicle will meet your budgetary needs and be a better choice than a more cheaply made vehicle with all the bells and whistles.

Also consider what will hold value better down the road. Oftentimes it's like buying a house. You may not need three bedrooms but you'd better buy that many, just for selling to the next guy. I'm not saying to buy just with the idea of trading, but at the rate people trade, you had better strongly consider it.

Just like spending thousands of dollars on fancy wheels and tires. If you do this just remember; you are buying these for your own use and when you trade it in, the next owner may not even care; you can bet the dealer won't. Certainly a dressed-up vehicle looks better, but you're fooling yourself if you think you'll get much more for it. Say you shell out three grand for a set of wheels, and the dealer will likely add anywhere from one hundred to five hundred more for trade value, if that! Used vehicle buyers are more concerned with mechanical condition and appearance than they are in gingerbread. If not, they'd probably be buying a new one.

I've taken in many, many vehicles over the years with the most sophisticated and expensive sound systems imaginable. In most cases, these sound systems were custom installed for that particular vehicle. The majority of buyers will splurge on this type of Installation only once in their lifetime and seem to outgrow the urge when they pass to the next purchase. Unfortunately, as previously stated, the next purchaser will likely not value the sound system as being worth any more to them than the factory setup. In fact, it often happens that they negatively refer to it as a *kid's car*; thus, assuming careless handling, poor maintenance and not a good investment. I've seen $6,000.00 to $15,000.00 sound systems that just bring no return in value beyond pennies on the dollar when they're traded in. Take the custom $12,500.00 system that I only allowed an extra $500.00 for, because its' speakers used too much space.

Certainly you can argue that kids couldn't afford that kind of expense, but it's a perception that has always been there. How many times over my career I've seen a six or seven thousand dollar sound system valued at the same dollar value of a factory premium sound system in the Kelley Blue Book. In other words, six thousand dollars invested returns three hundred to six hundred dollars at trade-in time. Honest, if you find a friend or a buyer on your own who can appreciate what you have invested; don't trade it in to a dealer. If you do, you'd better hope you paid cash for the system and could afford to lose that money, because you will. Many of these more expensive systems are still financed somewhere when they're traded in. Now you have a separate payment for nothing. The dealer gets the expensive equipment, and you get to keep making the payments, because it's part of the car. You lose!

If you do trade it to a dealer and if he does give you an extra trade value for your music system, then what you really ran into is a dealer who had a bigger markup than you realized and what you really got in essence, was a bigger discount. You still gave away the tunes. But the bigger discount went to making the stereo trade just look better so you could save face.

Have I belabored the point? I hope so! If you're going to spend money on a sound system, do it for your home. Don't throw your money away by putting anything but the basics in your automobile! Same goes for wheels and tires to a lesser extent. Again, I'll repeat; a purchaser of a used vehicle is far more concerned about the mileage and condition of a vehicle than how pretty the wheels are. Also, if you have low profile tires, this may mean the buyer will have to factor in the costs of replacing them anyway if he doesn't want the rougher ride. People add fancy extras for their own enjoyment, but these extras seldom add to your trade allowance!

Be very careful about how much you spend feeding your ego by spending excess money on a depreciable item such as a vehicle. Save the money, put it in the bank, and use it to pay into your next vehicle purchase.

So, take your time in the selection process and once you've done that, we can have some fun. That's right, fun! Because now you're going to be negotiating from strength rather than weakness. Now, you're going to win! Let's move on and see how.

CHAPTER 4
ARE YOU PREPARED TO NEGOTIATE?

Let's do a little *leg work* before we enter the arena. First, you need to know two things. One; an approximate dealer cost for the vehicle you intend to purchase, and two; the value in *wholesale dollars* of your present vehicle if you intend to trade it in.

Assume you are interested in a new vehicle. If you take a little time you can find out exactly what the dealer pays for it. This should be your first step. Your credit union or bank are likely to have access, either through their in-house broker or other personnel, to current dealer cost pricing on all new vehicles. You can also go to Edmunds.com and find invoice (dealer cost) on the internet. The invoice information that once was such a secret is now easy to obtain.

Just knowing dealer cost does not mean we can buy it for that, but at least we can now negotiate the amount of profit the dealer will make. Let's start with the factory price sticker, called the *Monroney label*, after the senator who influenced its' creation. A large number of dealers across the country will add a *supplementa*l price label alongside the factory price sheet. Oftentimes these additional labels are perfectly sized and colored so as to actually appear to be part of the factory sticker. Don't be misled. For the most part, these addendum (supplemental) stickers will have another dollar amount added, such as *ADP* (additional dealer profit) or *ADM* (additional dealer markup) or *AMV* (adjusted market value). However it may appear, it is still an additional price markup that the dealer will try to collect over and above the markup suggested as a fair price by the manufacturer. It may be explained to you that, "The factory has reduced the normal markup so as to make it too low for a dealer to survive on." Realize that no matter what you are told, disregard it! This is just an attempt to take advantage of you. If a vehicle is hard to get, the price will come down when it becomes plentiful, so unless you are desperate to be the *first kid on the block to own one*, don't pay the *boot*.

We are negotiating from cost and not from retail price, marked up or not! I want to elaborate here on this additional markup. There is only one reason for a price to be marked up on a vehicle without any service or equipment being added. Profit! Profit above and beyond the factory's suggested fair price

Remember this; history repeats itself in the automobile business. It never seems to fail that every time people are *paying through the nose* to have the very latest, within all too short a time, the production is increased and the demand is satisfied. Then, as also happens all too often, there becomes a surplus of that very same vehicle and the market is flooded. Then you find manufacturers giving rebates and dealers offering to sell them for invoice. Bottom line — There are too many good products out there for the average consumer to pay excess profit for anything.

If you have more money than you can spend or are in an income bracket where it doesn't matter what things cost, why not go for it? I doubt seriously that if money had no importance, you would be reading this book.

There is another factor in dealer profitability that I will now mention. This is the *holdback*. This is an amount, generally anywhere from 2% to 5%, of the invoice amount that a dealer receives from the manufacturer when the vehicle is sold. Even though it may not be in his hand at the time of sale, it is still income to him from the sale of the vehicle. Some dealers will even *dip into* this holdback when necessary to make a vehicle sell. Take the car that has been in inventory almost a year and still hasn't sold. A dealer wants it to go away, so he may well sell below invoice just to move it. At least he can stop paying monthly interest on it and free up room for more desirable inventory. He should be willing to sell it for invoice, minus holdback, and maybe a lot less, because every day it sits in inventory it costs him money! Also, in this day and age, the holdback will automatically be paid to his account by computer from the manufacturer. It is immediate. A dealer may argue that he has lost money on the vehicle due to interest he paid on it to keep it in stock (flooring) — too bad — not the buyer's concern! That is part of a dealer stocking inventory to be in business. Besides, if it hasn't sold for a long time, it's either unpopular, poorly equipped, the wrong color, or just a *butt ugly* car.

Internally, most car dealers have what they refer to as a *pack*. This pack is an amount which they add to the invoice which in effect raises their internal cost. This is an exaggerated cost which has no actual bearing on the true cost as far as the consumer is concerned. It is for dealership payroll purposes only. Salespeople are compensated on profits over and above this pack. Remember this when salespeople, managers and closers are telling you cost or showing you their computer cost printout which indicates a typed or written figure that they say is cost. They will explain that this amount marked up over invoice (pack) is necessary to pay the rent, lights, office personnel, etc. It's not true. It has no bearing other than a state of mind for dealership personnel to encourage higher gross profits and a shelter to enable the dealer to save commissions on this amount. Take a dealer who pays a 25% commission to his sales force. If his pack is $600.00, he saves $150.00 in commissions on each sale. The salesperson receives his 25% on any profit over and above this $600.00 pack. No matter what they show you, don't trust it unless you have a copy of the real invoice. A computer printout of an invoice can be quickly altered before printing, so be wary! Invoices also can be faked on the computer and I've seen people do it and show it to the customer, so when dealing on cars, you can't even trust what you see.

If you should buy a new car for exact dealer invoice, there would be no commissionable amount, and so it would actually appear to the sales department as a loss because of this pack. Regardless, the dealer will still pay the salesperson a minimum commission for a sale. There are a lot of dealers who advertise heavily on loss-leader vehicles actually at or far below invoice. Their salespeople work on these minimum profits and depend heavily on bonuses for certain sales levels. So the *no-profit* sale can be very important to them. Just because you plan to negotiate strongly, don't assume for a minute that they won't try hard to earn your business. For our purposes, let's not worry about anything other than determining the dealer's invoice price. For that, it's as easy as entering edmunds.com on the computer and price it out. I do not spend a lot of time worrying about the dealer's cost, as we are not so concerned about him making a reasonable profit, as we are about preventing him from making an unreasonable profit!

Now the second stage is to determine what your trade-in is worth. I'm not talking about *trade-allowance*, I'm talking *actual value*. So I don't mislead anyone, let's clarify this right now. The actual cash value of your vehicle is what it is worth on the *wholesale* market. Don't confuse this with trade-allowance, as we're going to negotiate a whole new way.

Trade-allowance as you are familiar with it, is the amount of money you receive for your vehicle from the dealer's list price or from the price you start negotiating at. This amount is made up of two factors. What your vehicle is actually worth (wholesale), and what a dealer will discount off the price of his vehicle.

Let's say for example, that your car is valued at a wholesale price of $10,000.00. Now say you're buying a vehicle that is retail priced at $30,000.00, and that it cost the dealer $26,000.00. He has a potential profit of $4,000.00 if he takes your car for its' actual worth of $10,000.00. If he gives you an $11,000.00 allowance for it, he makes $3,000.00 profit. I will cover a lot more of this in the chapter on Negotiating. Right now, just remember that we will not be concerned with trade-allowance, but rather with the wholesale value of your trade.

There are so many used car guides on the market that I will not list them all. Dealers use wholesale guides such as Blue Book, Black Book, NADA guide, Orange Book and numerous other guides as reference to determine the value of a vehicle. Different areas of the country use different guides and different lenders sometimes appraise for loans using different used car guide books, sometimes in the same city. These various used vehicle guides will not have exactly the same values for the same cars. Nor will all used car managers or appraisers come up with figures that are closely related. I've participated in meetings where different used car managers in the same city were asked to appraise the same dozen vehicles and I could not believe that we could vary so much in our valuations. Some appraisals were as much as $3,500.00 apart on the same vehicle, and these appraisals were done by highly respected used car managers and by dealers and general managers of dealerships who earned their living by accurate appraising. This was shocking to realize how inaccurate we were. This shows that used vehicle values are largely a matter of personal opinion when you are at the individual dealership level.

This example should put a person on guard. If you are shopping for an appraisal on your trade-in, can you ever afford to not get multiple appraisals? Using the fact we proved with our appraisal comparison, if you happened to hit the two extremes in your shopping, one manager would pay you $3,500.00 more for your trade than the lowest one. It sounds crazy, but like I said, appraisals are largely a matter of personal opinion based on the degree of knowledge held by the appraiser and his or her personal experience. Used car managers learn the hard way. If a car doesn't sell, they learn to take the next one in for less money. Experience is not easy to attain. Also, keep in mind that many used car managers will be conservative in their appraisals, as they would rather lose a sale, than pay too much for a trade, and others may be over aggressive in their appraisals in order to make more sales.

So how can you as an individual determine the value of the car you wish to trade in? A natural response at this point is, "Look at the Blue Book," etc. Certainly the most obvious, because all banks, credit unions, libraries, etc. have these valuation guides for your use. Be careful here, just because the Book tells you retail and wholesale values of your vehicle or trade value, don't for a moment think this is a realistic figure. These books are a guide and only a guide! Lenders use books to establish their guidelines for loaning money. Dealers use them for *reference*. In actuality, all vehicles have *value in relation to book*. Take the used luxury car that the book says has a wholesale book value of $32,000.00, but really is worth $27,000.00 (A.C.V. - actual cash value on the wholesale market). The used vehicles' true value is not a book valuation, but the actual price a dealer or wholesaler will pay for it. A lender though, will loan by whatever the book says in order to have a solid guideline to go by. Lenders cannot be experts in vehicle values, and that is why they base all of their values on a single source to maintain consistency. This all balances out in their loan portfolio, but a dealer cannot use these generalizations.

Most guide books reduce values in each issue by a percentage of the vehicles' original list price. We are all aware that a vehicle loses its most value the first year, and smaller percentages each successive year.

A car guide can't be that exact. Many dealers use auction reports to help determine values. Reports are sent out from dealer auto auctions that show what each vehicle sold for at the auction each week. These vehicles are sold by *dealers to dealers* and this reporting helps to more accurately determine wholesale values, because these cars and trucks are indeed being purchased for resale. Also, a used car manager needs to know that if he can't sell a vehicle to a retail purchaser, what he can auction it for.

A used car manager needs to know how a particular make and model appraises in relation to its' stated book value. Since the used car guides can't possibly reflect the changing market trends, and since they normally only decrease values by a given percentage each issue, the appraiser needs to know how each vehicle fares in relationship to its' stated book value. This is knowledge that can only be gained by experience.

If I call a competent used car manager on a particular car and he tells me it's worth a *nickel back*, that means that if I book out a car by adding the base book and all of its' options, then taking the mileage dollar addition or deduction, that I now deduct $500.00 from whatever the total is (a nickel is $500.00 back of (below) book).

Now, if he told me that a model is *bringing up money* that means it will be worth more than book (up). When a used car buyer says a vehicle is *soft*, that means it's not bringing near what the book says its' value is. Knowing the market is the key to a used car professionals' survival. In times of high gas prices, vehicles with large engines that guzzle gas lose value and the best mileage getters are going to bring *all the money.* Having a quick reference to a value (in relation to book) enables a dealer to add up all the options, and apply the *up-down* calculation to the total. As you can see, a used vehicles' value being so much a matter of pure, individual opinion, it pays to shop around.

Another factor that affects your value is need. It's always supply and demand in the used vehicle business. One manager may have a shortage of vehicles like yours, while another dealer may have several just like yours in stock, thus limiting his desire to take on another one unless he can steal it (own it for way less than what it's worth)!

Over the years, I found that different wholesalers in the same city had a wide disparity of buyers they dealt with in different cities. On many occasions when I was *shopping* (trying to sell it wholesale) a used car, I found buyers (wholesale dealers) who occasionally paid as much as $4,000.00 more for a car than all of the other bids I had. This is a huge difference in value, just by finding a dealer with outside connections. Professional wholesalers always know who buys what, and they have dealers they regularly sell to and buy from.

Some automobile dealers work with nearby wholesalers and have a very limited number of contacts. The dealer who has wholesale buyers he can contact in different parts of the country has a huge advantage, and is a benefit to the customer. For example, if you are trading in a two wheel drive Chevy Tahoe in Colorado, it's a benefit if your dealer has a contact in Houston that he can sell it to. If a dealer has to keep this sort of *odd ball* vehicle for his area, he will have to allow far less than its' value somewhere else, where people have no need or desire for a 4x4. Two wheel drive sport utilities are really plentiful in states like Texas, but are tough to sell in snow country like Montana!

Don't be fooled into thinking that you will get a higher value for your used vehicle by trading it to the dealer that you are buying the new car from. He may very well be selling to another dealer anyway. When times are slow, some dealers are in a financial position where they no longer can keep trades. Everything they take in has to have a home (be pre-sold) before they make a deal. This means that a dealer may have to wholesale every trade he takes, because he doesn't have the cash on hand to continue operating if he invests (spends) it on inventory that he must take in trade.

A quick note as to why. When a dealer takes in a car he must have enough cash on hand to own it, as the trades' value is that much less cash he takes in on the transaction. Say he sells a car for $30,000.00, takes a trade worth $10,000.00, when all money clears, he has to pay the bank off on the new car; let's say $28,000.00 and he receives $20,000.00 from you or your finance source. So now he has received $20,000.00 cash and a $10,000.00 trade, but he had to pay his bank (floor plan) $28,000.00 to release the title. His negative cash flow is $8,000.00 unless he has a floor plan line where he can floor the trade and put the $10,000.00 trade actual cash value (ACV) back in the bank. He then has a $2,000.00 positive cash flow.

In tough times, a dealer may have maxed out his used car floor plan, and his bank may have cut him off. Or maybe he just can't get the flooring line for his trades. Now he must have enough cash available to own the trade outright and still operate, or he must pre-sell every vehicle he takes in.

You will have no way of knowing, but if the dealer you're buying from is in this position, maybe the only wholesalers he can find to buy his trades are taking advantage of his situation. Maybe the wholesaler only offers him $9,000.00 for this trade. You see how that can affect your deal!

Now let's say the dealer has a used car manager who's a bit shady (happens a lot in the car biz). Same scenario, only the wholesaler pays the used car manager $10,000.00 for the trade, but the used car manager shows the wholesale amount at $9,000.00. If they then offer you $9,000.00, the used car manager shows the dealer that he sold the trade-in for $9,000.00 and you accept $9,000.00 for the trade, and the used car manager pockets $1,000.00. Either way, as a customer, you are getting less than you should for your trade. Now, if the wholesaler is really taking advantage of this dealer, you can see why it may really be advantageous to shop around. You may even happen upon the same wholesale dealer that the dealer uses, but to you, he may offer the same $10,000.00, and you win!

I highly recommend that you take the time to shop around for a buyer for your trade-in before you ever go to a dealership. Even if you owe money on it, a wholesaler will pay it off and give you the difference. I should mention that by wholesalers, you can go to any used car dealer, as they all buy cars. They can also put you in touch with other buyers (wholesalers). This is all easy to do, as it does not require any negotiating, and you may make a lot of money!

If you owe more on it than it's worth, you may have to make up the difference, but if you can pick up $1,000.00 or more over what a dealer would give you, it's to your benefit to figure out how to make it work.

So how do you determine the value of your vehicle? Well, here's where the effort to research properly may have you say, "I don't want to go through all of this, I think I'll just skip this part and take my chances." Isn't that what you've always done? For what it's worth; this is the best way to do it properly. I'm still going to save you a lot of money, so here's my suggestion: Visit some dealers who handle your make of car. Also visit some independent used car dealers; dealers who are not connected with a new car franchise, but have strictly a used car lot. Tell the used car manager or buyer that you are interested in selling your car. Tell them that you have already made, or are planning another purchase or a replacement so you are not interested in trading it in. Explain that you have the title, (even if you have a payoff) you can get the title and you just want to sell it to them. You may have to visit several or a great many dealers, but take the average of their bids and you will have an idea of what your car is worth. Don't be surprised or mad when the offers you get are well below the supposed wholesale number from the used vehicle guide books that you've looked at. Incidentally, look at the book first, so you'll see where they come in at if you care to, but book doesn't set the value, the market does. If a used car lot really wants your car, they will be willing to pay more than a dealer with several just like it in stock.

Another seldom realized fact is who your used car will most appeal to. Let's say that you own a Honda Accord. You have decided to purchase another one since you are happy with it, but just want something new. Who do you think will give you more money for it? Likely not a Honda dealer! Why? Because they are experts on their own products. They know what rebates they get on the new ones, what problems their used vehicles are prone to have, and since they have a high percentage of repeat customers, they most likely take in more Accords than they can use, so they may offer you much less than some other dealer.

Who? Almost any other franchise! Take Ford for instance. As a Ford dealer, my used car manager had to constantly attend the auto auctions to try to purchase import vehicles for our used car lot. All dealerships are in the same position. They quite naturally have their loyal, repeat customers, and to keep a good selection on their used car lot, they must be constantly buying competitive vehicles.

The general public falsely believes that dealers would rather have only their own used makes and models on their used car lots, and thusly think they can get a better deal by buying a Chevrolet from a Chrysler dealer and so on. Just the opposite is true, and for this reason, a good used car manager will try hard to buy every good selling competitive product he can. Now, when you go out to get your bids on your car, keep this in mind!

Another factor that works in your favor is that if you have a vehicle that look good and seems to be well cared for, a dealer will be more interested because he feels with a minimum safety check, he can put it right on the lot for sale, as timing is everything.

When you are out shopping around for *buy bids*, and you run into a dealer who has a *legitimate* buyer for your car and his bid is far above anyone else, you can always sell to him on the spot and then rent a car until you make another purchase. It happens a lot if you have a hard to get model, as a dealer may well have a *hot buyer* that may be willing to pay all the money for it, and you can both win big time.

Be prepared for some low starting figures, because any wholesaler will *try you on* by a low number on your car in hopes you may just grab it. No, you don't have to worry about negotiating; you are simply interested in getting a *bid to buy*. Make certain to ask; "Is that your best offer?" Also; "How long is it good for?"

If a buyer has an interest in your vehicle, he may very well need some time to make calls and shop it around. This is good business for a wholesaler because he can call many different dealers who sell your kind of vehicle, and he may be able to get you a lot more without your having to hassle with a trade-in to a dealer, and he can make some money for himself as well.

Now, a fact in your favor! Since used car managers are not that precise in appraisals and since they can vary so widely, there is a chance that one may mis-bid by quite a lot. But unless you've done the proper research, you won't know it if it happens and you won't be prepared to act on it. Don't be too concerned with great accuracy at this stage anyway, because even if you're way off on these numbers, the rest of this book will save you so much money that a few hundred dollars here or there won't matter to you anyway. Also, you can look in the newspapers and used car specialty magazines available everywhere. Get an idea what dealers are advertising vehicles like yours for. Remember, they should own them for less than they're asking, so allow for that, but again it's another reference source. Just be aware that ad prices are what a dealer is asking for the vehicle. He won't give *you* that amount.

If you're looking at buying a used car, use the same process. Look at guide books (making sure the guide you use is the one your bank or car dealer uses for your area. Also, visit a few dealers. Remember that you will see ads from private parties that are advertising their vehicles themselves because the dealer wouldn't pay them that much for it, so they hope to sell it for more on their own. So, they are likely priced higher than you will be offered by a long ways! Do not use private party ads for any kind of reference. In addition, I caution you to stay away from private party sales!

Keep in mind when you're asking used car dealers for *buy-bids* on your vehicle that they will hit you lower than they would really pay for it in the hope that they could steal it for less than its' actual value. You must be convincing when you are establishing the price a dealer would be willing to buy your car for. If you shop a used car dealer who does not own a new vehicle franchise, keep in mind that he may pay more for it because he won't have as many opportunities for taking trade-ins as would a new car dealer, and if it's a truly desirable car, he may very well pay more! Sometimes a lot more! This value difference will be an asset to you when you finally sit down to negotiate your deal. An independent used car dealer must buy his inventory from other dealers, private parties and auto auctions. In order for him to get good, clean, desirable vehicles, he must pay *up money*. You may get an offer that is a few thousand dollars more than you are offered for trade-in at a dealership. In addition, once you are in negotiations on the vehicle you wish to buy, if they will not meet the bid you already have from the wholesaler, you can produce his card, and they can call him to confirm that he will buy it. Now they can raise your trade allowance and know that they can sell it to your bidder; and you win! This way the trade amount comes directly off your balance owing, which makes it easier for financing.

I'll show you how to use this information to make your best deal in the Negotiating chapter.

All of this probably seems like a lot of extra work that you've never done before, but let's say you spend five to ten actual hours in research at the very most. You're likely to save between $1,000.00 to $5,000.00 by doing so. Do you currently make that much per hour? Look at it as a temporary, part-time job that pays exceptionally well, and the money you earn is tax free!

Remember, while you're doing your research and thinking that this is too much brain damage when you've always done well in negotiating before; the car dealer has his people train hundreds of hours every year in all types of selling scenarios. They memorize word tracks and practice role-play situations. They have answers memorized for all of your possible objections and sensible sounding reasons and documentation to back up every closing question they ask you. So you see, you really do need to prepare!

If you think you are ready to get in a peeing contest with a skunk, then go to it, otherwise continue to prepare. The good part of this preliminary work is that it doesn't create any challenge, or brain damage. No negotiating strain, or hassles, just friendly information gathering. Just a final word on the subject of shopping your trade. Let's say you find that independent car dealer who just happens to have a great inventory shortage, and he may offer you a huge amount for your vehicle. Now, when you sit down to deal on your purchase, you know that unless they exceed your bid, you sell to the other dealer. This can truly make you thousands of dollars, so don't cave in when the dealer tells you that you must trade your vehicle or he, "Can't get you financed." Just call the dealer you have the bid from and ask how soon you can get a check. If you trust the bidder, then you can give the dealer you're buying from your check in lieu of trade and ask him to not cash it until you deposit the wholesaler's check (This is the only time you should write a hold-check!). This should never be a problem.

CHAPTER 5
WOULD YOU BUY THIS CAR NOW?

Always keep in mind; as long as you have not signed the purchase documents, you are in the *driver's seat*. As soon as you give up the driver's seat, you then are open to be *taken for a ride*. Recognize the fact that everything in a car dealer's vocabulary includes the word *now*!

We give you many reasons why *now is so important*. They all are designed to imply either directly or indirectly that if you don't decide now, you will lose a great opportunity. Let's examine some of these tactics. Here are some examples:

"We need one more sale to hit our goal."

"My boss is one car short of his monthly goal and will do anything to make the sale."

"The owner calls every (any day of the week) and we must have a good day."

"I am just short of my bonus and will sacrifice my commission on this sale in order to hit my bonus."

"I have a new boss who needs to look good to the dealer, so he can make a better deal than I could get with another manager at another time."

"We report our sales to the factory by computer, and if we sell this one now, it means we hit our goal for allocation and the factory will build us another (one, two, etc.) right away. So this ends up being like a *free car* for us, as it won't count against our allocation, so we can really make a better deal for you."

"The other manager that works tomorrow doesn't give as high appraisals as the one working right now."

"The car you're looking at is scheduled to be sent to the auto auction and will be picked up by the trucks before we open in the morning."

"Another salesperson told me he has a customer coming in to buy this car tomorrow morning."

"We are reducing inventory dollars and today is the last day, because we've achieved our objective, prices go up drastically tomorrow."

"My boss just called his boss to see if we could make this deal, and he was told okay, but only because we can use one more sale today."

"We are only able to give you this trade-in value because we have a buyer for your car, but he wants it now or he'll buy something else. We need to commit to him over the phone. He's willing to buy it on my used car manager's word, because he's a long time customer and trusts us."

"I know that my boss made a mistake when he appraised your trade-in and he hasn't caught it yet, but by tomorrow he certainly will; then the value goes down."

"My appraiser just realized that he made a drastic error in the value of your trade-in, but since he quoted you this price, he feels honor-bound to live with it. However, if you leave now, it will give him a way out, and the deal is off. Don't miss the opportunity to take advantage of a car dealer."

"My manager has been in a sales contest with other sales managers in the state, and I just found out that it ends tonight and he's only one or two cars away from winning. That's why he's offering this to you at such great figures."

"The used car mechanic just came up to my manager and said your transmission has a bad problem. However, since my manager already agreed to these numbers, he won't change his trade allowance unless you leave; so basically, it's now or never. Let's not give him a chance to get out of it; shake my hand, quick."

"I just talked to one of the other salespeople and they called a customer, who's interested in buying your trade, but I must act now, or we'll lose the advantage of passing that retail price the other fellow will pay on to you as a trade-in allowance."

"My manager will be insulted if you don't take this great deal now and he will bow his back and refuse to do it later."

"Our incentive plan is over at midnight tonight."

"Interest rates go up tomorrow."

I'm sure if you've been around the block, you've heard some of these reasons to buy now. There are many more, but I made them up as I needed and tailored the reason to the situation.

I once witnessed a court action of a friend who was being sued by a customer because the BMW they purchased didn't come close to the mileage the salesman had promised. The presiding judge told the customer that misrepresentations like that are, "an accepted part of the car business," and he dismissed the case!

I draw the line however, at areas where flagrant abuse is concerned, such as where the customer needs to tow a 10,000 pound trailer, and the dealer sells him a half ton truck. I have terminated many salespeople over the years for lying and abusing customers. You should know by now, that you don't *have a friend in the car business*! Once you sign the papers and drive away, you own it!

If for any reason, you don't feel right about the deal, then *go home and think it over*! No matter how many stories they give you about *why you need to purchase now*, it's all bull! Just keep one fact in mind; there is seldom a true reason why an offer that's good today, could not be good tomorrow! The exception would be the legitimate ending of a factory rebate or interest rate specials that end at midnight, but you'd need to see it in writing.

Many customers take it as a personal insult by the dealership people continuing to negotiate for more money, but that's our job! I advise caution during these continued attempts to not turn hostile, because if I get the impression that you'll probably give us a bad rating on the factory survey, I'll end negotiations and say, "Goodbye" in a hurry!

Remember this, to a car dealer, any profit we can make is fair profit. As long as I don't misrepresent to you, and as long as I don't lie to you, I'll take all the profits I can get, without hesitation. The only exceptions that I personally have made are; elderly people, single mothers, mentally deficient people, veterans and those who genuinely can't afford much. If it will hurt an elderly person living on a fixed income, then I will back off. I think the majority of us have a conscience, but don't count on it. It's like being in a pool with a well-fed shark. He may let you pet him, but he could turn around and eat you just because it's his nature!

Is excessive profit making illegal? Immoral? No! Also, it may come as a shock to you, but lying in the car business is legal! That's right. Some lies are legal in the eyes of the law; it's called *puffery*, and puffing is acceptable, and as the previous example on lying about the mileage the BMW would get, the judge said, "It's okay to lie!"

We will do anything possible to make a sale now, because if we give most customers a chance to get off the hook after intense negotiating, chances are, we'll never see them again! Why, human nature. When both sides have negotiated hard to make a deal, they each likely gave more than they intended, and the dealer cannot afford to let the customer "Come out of the ether," as we say. The customers who take the time to go home and think about it rarely come back, and if they do return, they'll have a new offer for me! The customer who stays until we make a deal will usually pay a lot more than the one who goes home to think about it and then returns. Once the buyer is *under the ether*, we need to convince them to do it now!

As so often happens in negotiating, many customers will ask to see the book value. Now the dealer's people will just explain how book is only a reference point and that the book does not appraise cars. This part is true as we already know, but when a customer insists, they may produce either an actual book or a computer printout.

I will describe a favorite twist on this practice, and it works very well. Let's take an actual example of an incident involving what was at the time a *hot selling* vehicle. As so often happens in the *feast or famine* automobile business, there will be times when desirable vehicles may be hard to get. Factory changeovers, new models, or strikes; just one thing or another can produce stockpiles or shortages.

In this incident, the buyer was trading in a 4 X 4 Chevrolet Tahoe, and there was a nationwide shortage of new ones. He knew it, and since he was trading in a late model and buying a new Camaro convertible in the winter, he figured he was in the best possible negotiating position. He was fully aware that, to use the terms we already discussed, that used Tahoes were *bringing over book* (dealers were paying higher than wholesale book values).

When he asked to see the book, the sales manager printed a copy from the computer screen and the closer showed it to the customer. The buyer voiced his shock at how low the figure was, but figures don't lie; the closer made the deal, and they took in that Tahoe for a lot less than it was worth! What happened?

Had the customer thought to examine the printout more carefully, and read the ads on the margin where the Kelly Blue Book (in this case) sold advertising, he may have caught the fact that the dealer ads were for dealers in Phoenix, Arizona. The customer was buying in Minneapolis in January, and the Blue Book value was for the Southwest edition! That's right, you guessed it. A 4 X 4 Tahoe in

Phoenix was going to bring a whole lot less than it would in the Midwest edition! Conversely, a two wheel drive Tahoe in Denver would have been just as out of place and worth a whole lot less.

This is an old trick that customers never catch on to. Just for reasons like this, you cannot wait until you are in the midst of negotiations to do your research! You must enter the battle with a plan and the proper ammunition.

Keep it cordial. As a potential buyer, you will serve your own interests best if you exercise some patience. I know that it's hard to do when the person with whom you are negotiating seems to have not heard a word of what you said.

Keep in mind that no matter how much you preface your entry into the negotiating arena with your offer, the dealer still must try to get *all the money*. Can you blame him? Many people come on strong to begin with and lose all resistance quite easily. Unless they *try you on*, how will they know how strong you will be? Maybe you'll fold easy? Just hold your ground. You're earning their respect now!

Those of us in the automobile business live for the person who pays full price. That's how we make our money. If everyone that came in could buy at the lowest possible profit, people wouldn't stay in this industry! So keep this in mind when you are trying to buy a vehicle. Don't get immediately upset and threaten to stalk out, because losing your composure just shuts down the process. Some theatrics may be necessary but not too early in the game.

Just be aware that your first offer from the dealer will in most all instances be at the maximum profit for the dealer. Can you blame them? You need to repeat your position and send the offer back in to the sales manager. If you have done your research carefully and know that you have your figures correct, then stick with your offer. There is certainly no reason to compromise if you've done your homework. Just politely keep re-submitting your offer until they try to run the bluff and let you leave. You won't get far! They'll stop you at the door, or as you start your car the salesperson or manager will come running out to stop you. For that reason, always leave cordially and walk slowly. Part of the dealer's strategy is to *let you walk*. Don't worry; they'll stop you, if you're polite to them.

There are a couple of reasons why I say to maintain your composure when negotiating. I know it's hard to do because they do have a lot of people in their business who have simply terrible personalities. Just listening to someone who you can't stand is a chore, but put up with it as long as you can. The reason being is that most people in the business get to a point that if they are negotiating down to a minimum profit and the buyer is acting rude and abusive, they will oftentimes refuse the sale even though they could accept it if they wanted to. It's one thing to make a minimum commission on a person you like, but it's not worth it with an abusive customer. Have fun negotiating with me, and I'll give you a great deal, but get abusive, and I'll throw you out!

The dealer's main concern is that if you have an unfriendly attitude toward him now, what kind of response could he expect when you receive the survey mailed to you from the manufacturer. This is the dealer's *report card* which has a profound effect on his business. It also affects bonuses for all the sales force.

Just a note here to caution you that no matter how tough the negotiations get, you must let the dealer know that whatever went on before, you will still give them a perfect survey! People don't realize that a dealers' CSI (customer satisfaction index) is extremely important. Bonuses for salespeople and managers are predicated on perfect CSI more often than not. You must score them perfect if you purchase a vehicle!

I strongly feel that if you negotiate to an acceptable deal, that no matter how hard it was getting there, you still should fill out the factory survey as, "Completely satisfied." After all, if you make a deal, you have won. Don't be a sore winner!

Once, I remember after a hard negotiation, and making a deal I didn't want to accept, but I did so just to help the salesman, I remember the customer was still grumbling, so I stepped back in, and explained the importance of the survey, and asked for a good one. The customer replied; "I still think you could have made me a better deal, so I'm going to give you a failing grade!" I picked up the paperwork, laid his check back down, gave him his trade keys, and said; "Sorry, but we don't want your business," and I walked out. He tried to apologize, but I refused anyway. My salesman thanked me. He couldn't afford a bad survey, as it would have cost him a bonus which was greater than this small deal was worth.

I will not give you a good deal; even though you may have to work for it, and have you back stab me in the end. Remember, that somehow you need to impart this to the negotiator, so he or she will understand that if you win, they also win, no matter what goes on in between!

Equally important is, if they're only going to make a small commission on your purchase, don't expect them to put up with abuse. They don't need the grief! Their job is hard enough anyway and they don't have to put up with it. Also, salespeople appreciate gratuities! Don't be afraid to hand them some cash. Yes, many customers do tip their salespeople! Remember, you are going to be the ultimate winner!

Now let's get into the *working of the deal.* When the manager in the office sends his initial offer out to you with the salesperson or closer, we refer to this as the first *pencil.* This first pencil or offer is designed to test the water. They want to hit you hard to see how you react. Where they go next depends largely upon your reaction to this first pencil.

Look on this entire process as a play in which you have a major role. Stay in character and go through each scene, because as in a stage play, all scenes must play out in proper order before the act ends. You can make the play proceed faster, but give the dealer's cast a chance to say their lines. If they can't speak their lines, the next scene cannot happen, and the play cannot continue. It really is a lot like this when you are buying a car. Consider it a logical, progressive, stairway to the purchase. Go with the flow!

The sales manager must make his people do their trial closes and make all of the attempts shown in his scripted presentation.

Only after they have concluded all the pre-planned dialogue will the act end. If the play is interrupted by you not following your lines, it will be cancelled and you'll never get to the final act. Many dealerships are so structured that if they can't finish all their lines, they can't deviate until the script is read.

Go along with their attempts until they exhaust all efforts. Most of the time the closer is working harder to get the sales manager to take your deal than he is in grinding on you. Remember, he or she wants to make this sale, and they also wish to end the play; so stay cool!

Experience has proven that a dealer must make so many attempts at breaking your resistance to make sure you are not going to fold. Once all of their methods have failed, you can now take complete control, but you must wait until the right time.

Only when a dealer's game plan is exhausted, will he allow his managers to deviate. Time has certainly proven that with the millions of dollars expended by the automobile industry on sales strategies, that in the end of most presentations, the dealer will win! For this reason, we must let them run through their proven techniques in order to show them for sure that we are the exception to the rule. Now some dealers don't even play the game, so it may not even take all that long before you can take over and get the job done!

Consider a baseball game in the bottom of the ninth. The score is 10 to 0, and the team at bat just wants it to end because they have 0 and feel that they have no chance! They still need to take a minimum of nine pitches if they don't move, just so they can end the torture! Play ball!

Like I mentioned at the beginning of this book, many buyers just feel that if they are loud enough and forceful enough that they can intimidate their way to a good deal. I really enjoy these type of buyers, because I always compliment them on their negotiating skills, shower them with my praise on their tremendous bargaining, and once they are basking in their own glory, I usually make way above average profits! I mean like, huge!

You must understand that we car people have seen it all and done it all. We do this every single day, for 10 to 16 hours a day, and you won't beat us at our own game by just being obnoxious! We'll win every time, so please do your research!

I have made a great living all of these years, and have trained hundreds of managers and salespeople how to win! Now I will have the pleasure of teaching buyers to win, and let the dealers wonder what happened to their gravy train!

Does it seem like everything you must do to prepare for buying a new car is like running barefoot through the desert? Just too much work? Just when you think we've covered all the possible problems, you hear the music from the movie *Jaws* start to come over the speakers! Let's look next at the *SWITCH*! Oh yes, another scam that gets a high percentage of buyers. Has it happened to you?

Beware of the switch! While you are working intensely with the salesperson and the closer, the sales manager, who is desking your deal is busy trying to figure out if he or she can *switch you*! Yes, switch cars; convince you to buy a slightly different vehicle than the one you're negotiating to buy! Why?

Let's look at it from their standpoint: Let's say that you are trying to buy a new Chevy Camaro, and they are really pushing hard on how little your trade allowance is and how much more down payment and monthly payment you need to accept. Now suddenly, they casually toss out an idea as a, "What if I could," question. Such as, "What if I could sell you a fresh trade that we just took in that's almost exactly the same Camaro that you are looking at, but with only a few miles, and make it work at your figures? Now I don't know if I could even do it, but what do you think?" You may just be interested, and thinking you can't ever get the numbers to work on the new car, you agree to *look* at it. Now they go for the switch!

You are now shown the utmost care and consideration as both the closer and the salesman walk out on the lot with you, and as you go, they are conversing back and forth about how *nice the car is*, and how they hope they can make the numbers work! It's all a line of B.S! Of course they can make it work. All of this conversation is designed to make you want it before you even see it! They already know they can make the *numbers work*, because otherwise they wouldn't be leading you out to see it! Why both the salesperson and the closer together? Because they smell blood; a big gross profit! If they can switch you to the used car, the gross profit is, *going to the moon*!

So later, if they play it right, you drive away in a used Camaro after trading your car, paying the maximum down payment you can, and taking the highest monthly payment you can afford! You can bet that the salesperson, the closer, and possible the desk manager will all be out front waving goodbye when you leave. Friendly, right? No, they want to watch for the moment you drive off the lot, over the curb, and it's all yours! Their huge profits and commissions are now theirs to share!

The truth be known, you could have easily owned the brand new Camaro you really wanted had you known how to do the proper research! Certainly, the dealership would not have made the enormous profit they did, but they could have accepted what you offered. So why didn't they? Because you fell for the switch! That's why! Keep this in mind for the future; there is almost never a time when a dealer attempts to switch you to a different vehicle when it's for your benefit. It's always for theirs! They already know that they can sell you the one you want, and the switch is only attempted to make more money!

In our example, if you had refused to be switched to the used Camaro, you would see the other reason the closer accompanied you to see the used car. He has no interest in cars, and all the oohs and ahs are all an act. He is there in case you don't go for the switch, and if you decided to leave, then he would suddenly say, "I have an idea! I just thought of something that might work; follow me!"

Now he leads you back inside, instructs your salesperson to get you some more refreshments, and while you sit on the edge of your seats in anticipation, he's in the sales office saying, "Well, they didn't go for it, so give me another pencil." Now he comes out more excited than ever and tells you his *great idea*. Actually, his great idea has already been tried since you didn't go for the switch; he now has a much greater chance to get more profit from you!

How? Well you wanted the new Camaro; you negotiated hard, and lost all hope of buying it when they suggested you look at the used one. Your disappointment was heartbreaking when you lost your chance at owning your *dream car*! Now you have a chance at it once more, only now you will put more money down, accept a higher payment, and find any excuse necessary to justify your decision! How do I know this? It's human nature! Besides, I have performed this same act thousands upon thousands of times!

CHAPTER 6
FINANCE — THE SILENT DESTROYER

Now, we need to look at what could very well be the least understood and the most abused and costly part of the entire transaction!

Let's talk about what we refer to in the car business as *back-end* income. Profit from the sale of the car is *front-end* income, while profit in the financing of the car is referred to as the back-end. This is because we have two distinct profit centers. The front-end logically comes first, and this is where you decide what to buy and negotiate the deal. After the front, comes the back, and then you can go home in your new ride! Once the dealer has negotiated the best profit he can on the car sale, now he takes another shot at your wallet on the back-end! Just when you've relaxed, figuring the negotiations are done, you let down your guard and — Now when all you want to do is sign papers; they *start selling you* more profit-making products. To begin with, auto dealers are set up to *contract with you* for financing. You do not have to go to the bank; the dealer will do all of your paperwork in-house. If you read the fine print on the finance contract, it is generally, *between you and the dealer*. The dealer then assigns (sells) the contract to a lender and you make your payments directly to the lending institution. So the lender has no control over the negotiations or quotes. It's all between you and the dealer! Whatever the dealer charges you, as long as it is legal, is accepted by the bank. Do not be fooled into thinking that the lender has anything to do with what the dealer quotes you!

Lenders give the dealer the interest rate at which they will loan money based on amount, term and type of risk. The risk categories are normally determined by credit scores. The lender will typically allow a dealer to add at least 3% to this rate. The rate the dealer is given by the bank is called the *buy rate*. Let's say the buy rate is 8 ½%, but the dealer quotes you 11½%. The difference that you are charged is called finance reserve and is *additional profit* for the dealer. On a finance balance of $20,000.00 over a five year loan, this amounts to a difference in a monthly payment of $29.52 or a total over sixty months of $1,771.20. This is extra money the dealer just takes right out of your family budget. Now your credit may earn you a much lower rate than the example, but the dealer will still try to sneak in his full 3%!

If, however you have done your homework and you know that your credit entitles you to an interest rate of 4%, and if his buy rate is 4%, he still want to *capture* your finance business, even though he makes no profit; maybe a token paperwork fee from the bank is all. Why would he do the work for nothing? Protection!

The dealer cannot afford for you to go to your own lender because most banks and credit unions will also *take a run* at you to sell you credit insurance and service contracts (Yes, they are in the same con-game of selling you extra unneeded crap.), and if you had been duped into buying the service contract from the dealer, he risks having your own lender unscrew his deal and re-screw you with theirs. Can you see now that you can't trust your bank or credit union to not earn an extra commission by selling you things that benefit only themselves?

Rather expensive just to let someone do your paperwork, isn't it? The finance manager in a dealership is not a salaried clerk as you might suspect. Call them business managers, title clerks or what have you, (they use a non-threatening title), they are paid a percentage of what they generate in profit on your transaction. Why pay this enormous profit to perform a service that banks allow dealers to do as a convenience to the dealer?

You wonder why a bank allows a car dealer to take such advantage of you and still buy the loan? Profit! That's right; the bank makes a loan that the dealer has first shot at. If they don't have a program whereby a dealer can make his profits, the dealer will give it to a different bank. So, the *banker pimp* lets the *dealer whore* take advantage of the consumer to get more loans on their books. The reason they allow such a profit spread for the dealer is so they can be competitive with other banker pimps, in a market place with no limits on how much money is available to lend. Does it sound like you can't trust anyone? You are correct! Trust only yourself and be careful even doing that!

While you're having a tough time making your car payment because the payment is $30.00 too high, the dealer is taking the banker to lunch at the country club and wining and dining him to ensure their profitable relationship. Consumers never think about hating the bank for their payment problems, yet they're the ones who allow the dealer to gouge you in the first place!

Another item that they sell in the finance department is credit insurance. This is the insurance that pays the payments if you are disabled and pays off the loan in its' entirety if you die. Also, if you should purchase credit life insurance, keep in mind that this is a decreasing term policy, designed to pay off the loan balance. Don't let them tell you there will be a lot of money left over! This coverage is not mandatory and don't let them just sneak it in the contract. If you want credit life or disability coverage, buy it from your personal insurance agent. It's a lot less money. It is also a waste of money!

Additionally, you may be hit upon to buy an alarm system which has a great amount of built-in profit. Or the *ignition-kill gimmick* that the salesperson told you they put on their vehicles for the dealer's protection. The car can't be started without the gimmick chip and even though it's there for the dealers' protection, they might just *allow* you to purchase it. Wow, how generous! A two-bit cost item for between $200.00 and $400.00 profit (Watch this one close!). If it is on there, tell them to take it off. Don't just disable it, have them remove it! It is a complete waste of money and you're nuts if you buy it!

Now we get to the *fluff and buff* area. That's what we call the protection package that your vehicle must have to protect it against radioactive thermo nuclear acid rain and riots! Most of these protection packages include a paint sealant, an undercoating-sound deadener and interior protectant such as Scotchgard. They cost maybe fifty dollars to apply (including labor) and you may purchase them for anywhere from $400.00 to $1,500.00, depending on your level of resistance. Many of the products are placed over already factory undercoated and heat bonded lifetime interior Scotchgard (standard equipment from the manufacturer). So where is the need? This is another gimmick. I have taken so-called paint-sealed vehicles, and hand waxed vehicles and had them side by side on my showroom and there was no apparent difference. Don't buy any protection package! Period! The pitch often used on this one is, "It will enhance future value." This is a lie, and may end up costing you more if you ever have any paint work done on your vehicle. I have seen lots of cases over the years where body work cost a lot more and took longer because once an area was repainted, they had to wait and then apply a paint sealant to try and match what remained on the rest of the car so the colors would match.

I really wonder about people who regularly trade cars before the factory warranty expires, but finance for much longer terms to keep the monthly payments down. A high percentage of these people will buy service contracts! Why? Maybe because each time they really believe that this time they've found a vehicle that they'll keep longer? Whatever the reason, use more restraint in the future when it comes to the extras that you are *eligible* for *since you are purchasing from us*, this is another con statement. Beware of anything that you are eligible for. Also, use caution whenever you're told that this item is so special that you either go for it now or you'll never have another chance. Hogwash! Nothing is that special or that limited in the car business!

Be aware also of the rapidly growing *etch* business. Etch is another worthless gouge that you need to look for carefully. This consists of an almost undetectable number that is etched onto each glass panel on the car by a decal/acid process. The selling point here is the finance manager or salesperson will tell you that this number is used to identify your vehicle if it is ever stolen and parted-out by the chop shops. This number is supposed to aid police in finding and identifying vehicles that have been stolen because thieves wouldn't be aware of these secret numbers. Bull! They are etched in about two minutes of labor on the vehicle glass for the entire car!

They also tell you that you will be receiving a policy that covers you for a vehicle that is stolen and not recovered; they will pay you an amount like $2,500.00 to $5,000.00. This etch costs less than five dollars including labor and you will pay from $200.00 to $500.00 or more for it. Say no! Refuse this stupid rip-off. Some dealers will try to push you to buy it by telling you that they have to charge for it since it's already on the vehicle. Believe me, they can eat it! If they insist on charging you, leave. That type of dealer is someone you don't want to deal with anyway, and if they're that ruthless to push you on a two dollar *cost* item, they'll cheat you elsewhere also.

Let's look at a typical situation when you are meeting the dealer's finance people for the first time. First of all, you will have negotiated the sale to the very bottom line. You have the price where you feel it's fair and have received what you feel is equitable for your trade-in. The monthly payment, although not where you'd hoped, is one you can cope with. Now you are introduced to the *business manager* who will do your *title work*. Now, after some of the same disarming and warming up conversation that you wade through in the car-buying process, you must again be prepared to make buying or non-buying decisions. Be careful here! Very careful! This is the point where you are the most vulnerable and where you are most easily conned! Do not ever shake hands on a deal where all you know is the monthly payment!

I will cover much of this process in the Negotiating chapter, but the end result of working your strategy *strictly on payments* can and *will* cost you money in the finance department! Go along with me for a minute and assume that all negotiations on the car were okay and you feel that the payment of $400.00 a month is acceptable. Now, let's just assume that if the sales manager had wanted to, he could have quoted you a payment based on interest buy-rates available to him, and with your credit rating, of $350.00 per month. This difference between what we could do and what we had you agree to is referred to as *leg*. Assuming that as in a typical transaction, you haven't been told what the interest rate is, but only that, "Gee I don't know, but our business manager will go over all of those details with you."

Now the sales manager *structures* this deal for the finance manager to be able to maximize the profit for the *house*. The business (finance) manager now enters into the pitch on the service contract and although you're interested, you feel that $400.00 per month is your limit on what you can afford.

You have worked your entire sale based on monthly payments, so you really have no idea that the finance manager has a *packed payment* to work with. He or she knows that the sales manager has given them a gift, at your expense, of $50.00 per month! Since you are prepared to sign papers agreeing to that payment, unless they can sell you something extra to finance, they will have to lower your monthly payment back to $350.00! No, the payment buyer never sees this happen, because he's too easily bilked!

Now they continue to push this service contract, even though they could include it at no additional monthly cost; they cannot arouse your suspicions, but must continue to sell the benefit, and once you ask how much it costs, a miracle happens! Because you are such a nice person, they can include the deluxe $2,800.00 service contract for a mere $10.00 extra per month! Your new payment is only $410.00! Congratulations!

At this point, I will state unequivocally, so that there is no doubt that I recommend that you should *NEVER* purchase a service contract (extended warranty) on a new vehicle! *NEVER!* However, for purposes of explanation, using this example, let's say your balance to finance is $25,000.00. You add a service contract for $2,800.00, finance for 6 years (72 months) at an interest rate of 7%. By financing this service contract on top of your vehicle, you will pay an extra $637.00 in interest, bringing the cost of the service contract to $3,437.00. All of this extra is unnecessary when you consider that when your warranty is close to being up, the factory will offer you a *manufacturer's extended warranty* and allow you to pay for it monthly at zero interest!

But wait! Hold everything! Does it not seem strange that $2,800.00 financed for five years only raises your payment by ten dollars a month? Sixty months times ten dollars equals $600.00. That is at zero interest. How doooo they do it? It's funny how the average *payment buyer* will not even think rationally at this juncture that something must be wrong! The finance manager could include the service contract and still lower your monthly payment, but the small bump up to $410.00 per month still leaves some leg in case you will buy something extra, such as etch!

Are you starting to get the picture? You may not be one of the 32% of the people who buy this way; so count yourself lucky! For the unfortunates who have had these experiences, what happens now? Let's say in this scenario that there is nothing more the buyer will purchase. The finance manager must now disclose all of the figures. He or she still has a buyer who agreed to a higher payment than the law allows. There is too much remaining leg! The *miracle* must also be explained. How did they sell you a $2,800.00 service contract for ten dollars a month, and now after that, the new payment went even lower! It is now $398.00!

Remember that this is a *true payment buyer*! They have never discussed numbers or rates, just payments! It's a simple matter now to explain, "Our dealer really helps our customers in every way he can. In your case, and because of your good credit, he was able to talk the bank into lowering your interest rate and so basically, you're getting a free warranty and still a lower payment!" What a wonderful dealer! The dealer doesn't even know these people exist, but it certainly sounds good.

You think this scenario sounds unrealistic? Thirty-two percent of you don't! I made an exceptionally high income for 40+ years working with payment buyers. These people really have a lot more fun in their transactions because there is never a hassle; the dealer's people treat them as V.I.P.'s, and indeed they are! I will repeat again, "The payment buyer is God's gift to the car dealer!"

So you see by not knowing how to work out your true monthly payments, you leave yourself open to succumbing to these extras because they cost almost nothing to include. Even though it's illegal, you still have finance managers who will tell the interest-rate conscious customer that, "If you buy the fully protected payment (insurance coverage), the banks will allow us to lower the interest rate and so basically, you are not paying at all for the additional benefits!"

You see, if a finance manager has let's say $50.00 a month in leg, he would rather use it to sell you the extras such as insurance, protection packages, etc. rather than just leave the extra profit in interest rate. The reason being is that when you buy these extra products, should the finance contract be pre-paid, the dealership keeps their profit. On the other hand, if all of the extra profit is due to a higher interest rate, and you refinance later on to attain a better rate from some other lender, then the dealer does not receive the *finance reserve* (excess) from the bank. Finance profits are only paid as a share as long as the finance contract is ongoing. Knowing this, a dealership is always cautious with credit-worthy individuals because if they overcharge by too much, a customer will go to his own financing source and pre-pay the loan. This, they don't want. People who have the least desirable credit ratings however, are the least likely to shop around for cheaper money and generally are gouged quite heavily in finance profit. So, they prey on the poor and make them poorer! The sad part of it is that so many people with good credit are duped into believing they do not have good credit, and are therefore susceptible to the con.

The following *factor chart* and a calculator are all you need to calculate monthly payments. We'll be using this chart as we travel through the Negotiating chapter. Understand it thoroughly and use it until you feel at home with it. Nothing is more unnerving to a salesperson, *closer,* or finance manager than having a customer who is able to calculate his or her own payments.

This chart is the major key to saving you thousands of dollars!

Let's examine our chart.

APR		NUMBER OF MONTHS					
	24	30	36	48	60	72	84
4.00	0.04342	0.03508	0.02952	0.02258	0.01842	0.01564	0.01367
5.00	0.04387	0.03553	0.02997	0.02303	0.01887	0.01611	0.01413
5.50	0.04409	0.03575	0.03019	0.02325	0.01910	0.01634	0.01437
5.75	0.04421	0.03586	0.03031	0.02337	0.01922	0.01645	0.01449
6.00	0.04432	0.03598	0.03042	0.02349	0.01933	0.01657	0.01461
6.25	0.04443	0.03609	0.03054	0.02360	0.01945	0.01669	0.01473
6.50	0.04455	0.03620	0.03065	0.02371	0.01957	0.01681	0.01485
6.75	0.04466	0.03632	0.03076	0.02383	0.01968	0.01693	0.01497
7.00	0.04477	0.03643	0.03088	0.02395	0.01980	0.01705	0.01509
7.25	0.04488	0.03654	0.03099	0.02406	0.01992	0.01717	0.01522
7.50	0.04500	0.03666	0.03111	0.02418	0.02004	0.01729	0.01534
7.75	0.04511	0.03677	0.03122	0.02430	0.02020	0.01741	0.01546
8.00	0.04523	0.03689	0.03134	0.02441	0.02028	0.01753	0.01559
8.25	0.04534	0.03700	0.03145	0.02453	0.02040	0.01765	0.01571
8.50	0.04546	0.03712	0.03157	0.02465	0.02052	0.01778	0.01584
8.75	0.04560	0.03723	0.03170	0.02477	0.02064	0.01790	0.01596
9.00	0.04568	0.03735	0.03180	0.02489	0.02076	0.01803	0.01609
9.25	0.04580	0.03746	0.03192	0.02500	0.02088	0.01815	0.01622
9.50	0.04591	0.03758	0.03203	0.02512	0.02100	0.01827	0.01634
9.75	0.04603	0.03769	0.03215	0.02524	0.02112	0.01840	0.01647
10.00	0.04614	0.03781	0.03227	0.02536	0.02125	0.01853	0.01660
11.00	0.04661	0.03828	0.03274	0.02585	0.02174	0.01903	0.01712
12.00	0.04707	0.03875	0.03321	0.02633	0.02224	0.01955	0.01765
13.00	0.04754	0.03922	0.03369	0.02683	0.02275	0.02007	0.01819
14.00	0.04801	0.03970	0.03418	0.02733	0.02327	0.02061	0.01874
15.00	0.04849	0.04018	0.03467	0.02783	0.02379	0.02115	0.01930
18.00	0.04992	0.04164	0.03615	0.02937	0.02539	0.02281	0.02102
20.00	0.05090	0.04263	0.03716	0.03043	0.02649	0.02395	0.02221
22.00	0.05188	0.04363	0.03819	0.03151	0.02762	0.02513	0.02343
25.00	0.05337	0.04516	0.03976	0.03316	0.02935	0.02694	0.02531
30.00	0.05591	0.04778	0.04245	0.03601	0.03235	0.03008	0.02859

A factor is simply a multiplier we can use to determine a payment based on a known interest rate for a particular term. For example, let's say we wish to finance $10,000.00 for a five year loan at an interest rate of 10%. Go down the left hand side of the chart until you find 10%. Next, go across the top of the chart to 60 months and where the two columns intersect, you find the *factor* to be .02125. Multiply this factor times 10,000 and your payment is $212.50 per month. Let's try another one; Say you wish to budget for a payment of $350.00 per month and you are willing to finance for a period of not more than four years. Wanting to stay in-budget, you want to know what price range you can shop in. You feel you can get financing through your credit union at 8% A.P.R. (annual percentage rate). Go to the 8% column on the left of the chart. Slide over to the 48 month column and you find the columns intersect at .02441. Now, divide $350.00 (your budget) by .02441 and your answer is $14,337.21. You know that if you borrow this amount at an interest rate of 8%, your monthly payment will be $350.00.

Try another one; you decide that the car you like is $18,000.00 but the payments on this amount at a 9% rate over 60 months will run $373.68 per month. Again, intersect the 9% and 60 month columns and the factor is .02076, multiplied by $18,000.00 equals $373.68. You really want the car but can only afford a maximum of $335.00 for your budget. How much cash down or trade-equity will you need for this payment? Divide $335.00 by the factor of .02076 and we get a balance of $16,136.80. Since this is what we can finance to hit the payment we want, then it will be necessary to reduce the $18,000.00 balance by $1,863.20 to stay within budget. As we go, we will refer back to this chart to see how car dealers *work the deal.*

I highly suggest that before you ever attempt to start negotiating that you first sit down with your bank or credit union and get pre-approved for financing.

Keep in mind that you may even be able to negotiate with your lender! When they tell you the rate and term at which they will lend you money, it is always to your advantage to just look them in the eye and ask, "Can you get it lower for me?" They may not, but oftentimes they will, in order to get the loan! Try anyway, it costs you nothing, but may just save you money!

Let's say your bank says they will give you a loan at 5.75% for up to 72 months. Ask how much it would cost to borrow $1,000.00 at these terms. They will tell you $16.45 per month. Now, look at the factor chart and you'll see how it works. Write down .01645, and carry it with you. Now whenever you need to calculate, multiply that number times the balance to finance; this will be your monthly payment.

Now, for an alternative way to calculate your payments that will require a calculator and a few more steps, but you won't need a chart. Multiply the principal balance $ (amount financed) by the interest rate % as a decimal. For example, an interest rate of 6.5% would be entered as .065, 7.25% would be .0725, etc. Divide the balance by 365 and multiply the new balance by 17 and multiply that new balance **X** times the number of **M** months to finance. Add **+** this number to the $ principal balance and divide the total by the number of **M** months financed and you have your approximate payment.

$$\$ \times \% \div 365 \times 17 \times M + \$ \div M$$

$ = Amount Financed

% = Interest Rate

M = Months Financed (Term)

So, you take the amount financed times the interest rate, divide by 365, multiply by 17, multiply by the term plus amount financed, divided by the number of months.

Write this formula down and keep it with you. Amount financed x % rate, ÷ 365, x 17, x months + amount financed, ÷ months. Let's look at an example. Say we are looking at a balance to finance of $27,000.00 at an interest rate of 6 ½% and we want to finance for 60 months. Our formula should be 27000 x .065 ÷ 365 x 17 x 60 + 27000 ÷ 60. When we do this as a continuous calculation, we get a monthly payment of $531.00. This formula will give you a payment within a few dollars of the one derived from using the factor chart. Either one you use, make sure you periodically check the numbers shown to you as you are negotiating the deal

If you have caught your salesperson in a lie, there is a good chance either he, or his manager has *packed* the payment. If you catch a discrepancy, bring it to their attention and if they give you the story that, "The computer just figures it approximately," or some other reason such as, "The computer probably calculates the payment including the credit life and disability insurance," or some other line of bull, bring it to their attention and ask that future calculations be made exact and without extras. Computers do not calculate things approximately! They do it exactly. If they tell you different, they are pulling your leg (lying)!

When a salesman or manager is working with you on a car deal they will keep quoting payments even though you may have told them that it wasn't an important part of your decision. They do so to keep testing the water. They want to see how you react, knowing that if they can get you discussing payments, their job will be easier and the profit margin greater once you become a payment buyer. Therefore, every change in figures will be accompanied by the *payments bait*.

If this inexact method of dealing is not immediately corrected, and your calculations show they are persisting to lie, then leave! If you recognize the warning signs, and stay for more, you deserve what you get. When you ask the salesperson or manager what rate they are using to calculate payments, they should be able to tell you. If not, then watch out! A lot of dealers and their representatives will tell you the *system* calculates payments based on an *average rate*. Well, the computer doesn't do this on its' own, someone must enter an interest rate, so don't listen to that line of bull! Insist on knowing what rate they are using to calculate the payments they are offering you. You should already know what rate you can qualify for anyway (from your own lender), so tell them to use that rate to calculate the payments. Then, when they do, check them with your calculator to make sure they're taking you serious. It is best you don't even rely on their calculations anyway. Just do it yourself as you go. They won't mind, as they would do the same if they were buying a vehicle (if they knew how).

Let's go back to the case I mentioned previously where the buyer could afford and agreed at to a monthly payment of $400.00. Cutting out the excess leg, we saw that the dealer could, in reality, have sold the car for $350.00 per month. Now what if the bottom line was realized by the customer by calculating their own payments up front? Could we not then assume that an extra $50.00 per month on a sixty month basis would purchase another $2,800.00 worth of car? Perhaps the customer could get the next model up with over two thousand dollars more equipment and all for the same payment! If you aren't prepared to calculate your own payments, then you're just asking to be *skinned*. You may also be looking at less car than you really want, and can afford. This step alone will change your car buying forever!

As I previously stated, part of your preparation before buying a car should be to ascertain what interest rates and terms are available to you. If you belong to a credit union, find out their rates and terms. Your bank will also be a good source. Tell them you're looking at cars, and if you have doubts as to what rate you can qualify for, then pay their credit check fee and see if they will pre-qualify you. Most lenders will pre-qualify you at no charge. If you have marginal or poor credit, don't just take the dealer's word for the rate they say you must pay. Let's say that your bank will lend you money for 6% and for a term of six years. Your factor is 6%, 72 months = .01657. Carry it and calculate your payments.

People who have had poor credit are used to paying higher rates, but oftentimes they can quality for a lot lower rate. So many people with a few glitches in their past are continually mistreated and cheated because they really are embarrassed to go to their own lender and seek advice. They find that dealing directly through the car dealer is so much easier, and the car people really treat them well. Of course they do, and they're paying thousands of dollars extra on each transaction to be treated nicely. You deserve better!

One of the negotiating skills the salespeople practice on is to identify with the customer. If you indicate that you have a credit problem, they will immediately respond with, "Me too!" One of my favorite salesmen was so practiced with putting the customer at ease, that when he sensed his customer may have credit issues, he would disarm them by asking, "Do you have real good credit, or credit like mine?" They would respond with, "Credit like yours!" Automatically assuming he had bad credit, and an immediate bond was formed! From that moment on, they were family!

Always remember that salespeople are trained to schmooze you! You can't very often discern reality from acting, because they earn their living by practicing many hours every week in the *art of the con*!

Unfortunately in our system, the disadvantaged are held down and taken advantage of big time. It is so tragic to see so many nice people screwed over by car people when the obnoxious, know-it-all, with good credit gets all the breaks. The big partner in all of this crooked dealing is the professional and so innocent looking bank! That's what I said; the bank or finance source that enables the dealer to make these excess profits.

Does this sound like a lot of work so far? Would you rather just get right out and shop for cars? If you had enough money that you didn't care, then you wouldn't be reading this book in the first place. So continue along, as you are learning skills here that will save you enough money over your lifetime of car buying to equal the price of at least one new car *free* out of ten purchased. Sound crazy? Figure you buy at least ten cars over your lifetime. The average is probably closer to twenty-five. Save at least $1,000.00 to $2,000.00 on the purchase, save another $1,000.00 or so on financing, save another $500.00 to $1,000.00 on worthless rubbish like paint sealant, warranties, and junk you may never use; you add it up! $1,500.00 savings on the purchase, $1,000.00 on financing, and $500.00 on junk = $3,000.00 x 10 cars - $30,000.00 savings.

For purposes of simplicity, I am going to leave out any inclusion of sales tax and licensing in our calculations, because it's there no matter what.

Most states will charge a sales tax based on the difference between the cost of the vehicle you're buying and the trade-in, since you've already paid tax on the trade when you bought it. There are some states however, that calculate tax differently, so make certain you know your state tax and licensing laws. Don't allow yourself to be conned by the dealer into thinking that you have plenty of time to pay the state. You won't have! If you buy in a state that doesn't charge sales tax and you live in a state that does, you will have to pay it to license it! And, you must do it immediately! No grace period!

Another reason that I'm not including the tax and license numbers in the text is that I hope you can pay these amounts in cash and not finance them in your contract. If you are not financially able to pay the tax, then calculate it in by adding the amount to your balance to finance and use the factor chart to calculate your payment, including the T & L.

Do, find a way to pay cash for your license however, or you'll end up financing it in and end up paying interest for years on one or two years' license renewal. This is just more expense you must try to control.

Understand that I know there are many car buyers without the ready and available cash to do this, but unless you desperately need a vehicle because your other one blew up, or some such mishap, maybe you shouldn't be buying at this time.

Look at it this way, if you are only trading because of desire, and not out of an absolute need, and you can't pay cash for the tax and license, then you can't afford to trade! Keep what you have, save money, and buy when you can better handle it.

Now let's talk about re-signs. It's common practice in most areas for dealers to perform *spot deliveries*. This means that they will have you transact the entire sale; financing and title work and deliver you on the spot. Even though your financing may not have been approved, you will sign a finance contract that is a generic form, so depending on which bank gives final approval on your loan, they can send it to that bank without having to have you come in and re-sign.

In some cases the lenders will refuse to accept the contract until certain conditions are met. When this happens, you will receive a call from the dealer asking you to come in and sign paperwork for a different bank, or maybe a change of term, interest rate or any number of reasons.

Watch out here! Anytime they tell you that they need you to re-sign, that generally means that none of their lenders accepted your contract as submitted; which in turn, means that conditions are going to change. You're saying "Oh, oh," but don't despair, this can work to your advantage if you play it right!

Whenever you are asked to re-sign papers means that something is going to change. You're correct if you assume that something is changing that will not be to your benefit. I'm going to give you a true story that a customer shared with me, that happened to him and his wife.

These folks had a completed a long and strenuous negotiating session that lasted for hours. Throughout the time, their salesman, let's call him Ted, remained super-pleasant and whenever the closer was out of the tiny closing booth, he expressed his apologies for what they were going through. Ted was doing his job in the good guy, bad guy strategy, and reminded them of their grandson, so they developed a certain bond with him although they hated the closer.

Finally, it all ended and they bought the car, with apologizing from Ted all the way; they really formed a close relationship. That evening they had just finished dinner when the phone rang and it was Ted. He sounded in tears, and when the lady asked what was wrong, he poured out his story. He said, "After you left, I was taking your paperwork over to our administrative office, and since it was raining, I jumped in my car to go, and without realizing it, I dropped your contract on the ground and backed over it with my car! Now my boss said he is going to fire me because the paper is worthless!"

The customers were very sympathetic and told him, "Ted, you bring over new papers right now, and of course, we'll sign them!" Ted was there quickly, and as evidence, produced their papers, and sure enough, there was a wet tire print directly across the contract. They gave him their other copy to take back, and when he produced the new contract it had x's marked for them to sign; which they quickly did without questioning it, and without reading it. Ted was even so courteous as to fold up their copy and put it in the envelope with the title work that their other copy had been in. He handed back the envelope, chatted for a while, and even talked about their grandson the he reminded them of, and then he left.

After that, the folks enjoyed their new car, until the day they received their payment book from the bank. Then the bomb went off! The payments were sky high! They ran for their papers, and whoa, there was an additional five thousand dollar increase on the sale price from what they had agreed to! Naturally, there was no proof of any other figures; remember, they had given their original copy to Ted. When they tried to sue, the judge made the dealership produce the papers; there were no scratch paper sheets that they had originally worked with. Just the papers they had signed when the salesman had come to their home. The salesman and the manager denied ever having discussed any other numbers and the salesman swore he had never been to their house! Case dismissed! They paid the money! Just be careful before you re-sign anything!

Keep one thing in mind if a re-sign situation happens to you, and don't forget it! Whenever there is a necessity for re-signing a finance contract, there are most often only a couple of reasons. Reason one, the interest rate the dealer calculated was incorrect and he has to change it for the lender to accept the loan. Staying with reason one for a minute, two possibilities occur here. Either he didn't charge you a high enough rate or he charged you too much. Yes, too much! Not that banks have much of a conscience, but there are usury laws!

Well, if he didn't charge you enough, he will tell you just that. Ask to see the paperwork from the lender to verify this. Why I suggest you make this request is, because while true, he may be trying to pick up more profit from you. Let's say for example that he thought the buy rate (percentage the dealer pays the bank) for your loan would be 10% APR and he charged you 11%. He makes this difference of 1% as a profit. The bank tells the dealer that they want a buy rate on your loan of 12%. So now he really must have you re-sign. Once he calls and you agree to stop by, he knows by now that if you're coming in to re-sign, that you really love the car and want to keep it so he may just tell you the rate changed to 14%. If you re-sign at that rate, the dealer now makes a 2% profit and you pay much more than necessary.

Now turn this situation around. Say the dealer was charging you 14% up front and the bank rejects the financing because the rate is too high! This happens all the time. What generally happens in this scenario is the dealer feels you qualify for a 9% buy rate and he writes your finance contract at 14% hoping to make the 5% difference as a profit. He reads his guidelines incorrectly, because the bank only allows him a 3% increase over buy rate on this particular loan, so he must re-sign or the bank won't accept the contract.

The dealer gets you in to re-sign, but here's where good news changes to either lying and selling, or just plain lying. He's not going to be honest with you by admitting he was being too greedy. He will tell you that he really worked on the bank and convinced them that you're such a good customer that they should lower your interest rate and they agreed. Now you're told how lucky you are because, "With the lower rate you can get that service contract you wanted and your payment won't change." Or the real big lie; "If you buy a service contract the bank will lower your rate so your payments won't go up because the bank will feel better knowing the vehicle will be protected." This is not only a lie; it's also against the law! But, these scenarios happen every day! This makes it easy for the dealer to sell you the item you couldn't afford by stealing your money to pay for it!

The second reason you may be called to come in and re-sign is that the bank won't advance the amount the dealer is trying to obtain on your contract. Now you're going to be asked to come up with additional down payment. They're going to tell you that the bank wants more money down. When they do this, let's remember that the door may have just opened for further negotiations on your car deal! That's correct; this may be your opportunity to get an even better deal!

Put yourself in the dealer's, or better yet, in the managers' position. He or she has sold and spot delivered you in a vehicle that has now come out of inventory, out of the computer, out of mind, and possibly in the case of a new vehicle, the title work has maybe already been sent to the state. Likely the sale has been triggered to the manufacturer and the warranty started, and must now be resold as a used vehicle if you give it back; or maybe it was the last sale needed for thousands of dollars in a dealer contest. This actually happens! There are many repercussions when a dealer *unwinds* a sale. When a dealer rescinds a sale, they unwind it. Unwinds are bad for them because the salespeople, closers, sales managers, and finance manager all stand to lose commissions. Even if profit goes down, we still count the sale towards unit bonuses and even if all of the profit goes away, the salespeople and their managers still get paid a minimum commission. In addition to that, the managers must answer to the general manager or dealer for why it bounced back! For dealers who own multiple franchises, all of their managers are in competition for sales numbers. The loss of any sale sends up a flag. A really negative flag regarding the judgment of the manager who *rolled* (spot delivered) the vehicle.

So you see unwinds are bad, bad! But for you, they may be good, good! This fact puts more bargaining chips on your side of the table. Now when presented with the fact that the bank wants more money down, handle it this way: First, tell them that you have no way to come up with any more money down. If they offer to take payments or *hold checks* for a later date, it's a good sign! That means that they can probably live without it because a high percentage of buyers never make good on these future promises anyway, and the dealer knows that by offering this option, he may never see his money, and if so, he can live without it. If he gets it, it's all gravy.

If this vehicle is one that you'd really like to keep (unless buyers' remorse set in already), then run the bluff by saying, "I guess we'll just have to give the car back." Maybe if it works out that way it's for the best anyway, because the additional money down may create a financial hardship for you. So, offer to give it back and see what they say. Go as far as to have them prepare the return paperwork. Also, they may have already let a wholesaler pick up your trade, so they can't give it right back (unlawful). If they cannot produce your vehicle to trade back, they are in a position where legally, they will be stuck! They are now likely to eat the difference needed in down payment. By law, if they can't make the deal, they must immediately hand you back your trade-in. No delays are granted!

In most cases where we're not talking a large amount of additional money, the dealer will agree to waive it. Now your price goes down. Now you can re-sign, but make sure the interest rate stays the same as it was and check to make certain that nothing else such as the etch, protection packages, or service contracts have been added.

I've seen a lot of these re-signs where the customer has such trust in the dealer after a situation like this occurs, that they just sign whatever is put in front of them. The fact they may have given up some profit to keep the sale together does not mean that you can't refuse to be taken advantage of. If they hadn't led you to believe the financing would be approved, you likely wouldn't have taken delivery of the vehicle in the first place. Dealers push really hard to make sure you *drive it home.*

This brings up one of the oldest tricks in the book. A dealer knows that the bank won't accept the finance contract as it is written. He sends you home allowing you to think you are all approved. You show your new car to your friends, neighbors, and coworkers. You're happy with your new car. Then, the dealer calls you and says, "We've got a problem." He knows that once you've shown your new car to the world that you'll now do whatever it takes, within reason, to retain ownership and avoid the embarrassment of having to give the car back! Rather than suffer this humiliation, people will jump through a lot of hoops to come up with more down payment. This is one of the more common dirty tricks in the car business. Knowingly sending a customer home and then changing terms afterward is a crummy way to make money, but it's all part of the game.

Another caveat is that in the case where the dealer simply can't get the financing and you have to return the purchase. If you had a trade-in, make sure you get it back in the same condition and with the same equipment it had when you traded it in. Also make certain that before you surrender the dealer's vehicle to him that you receive everything you gave him including title, registration, license plates, any money you put as down payment, extra keys, etc.

What happens if the dealer has already sold your trade-in? Now you've got him! If he cannot produce your trade-in, you don't give his car back.

I remember so many cases like this, but some just stand out. One for instance, was a case where the ACV (actual cash value) of the trade-in was $4,000.00, but the dealer, in order to make the contract look good to the bank, raised the selling price by $4,000.00 and showed a trade allowance of $8,000.00 to the bank. The financing fell through, but the dealer had wholesaled the trade-in and the wholesaler had already sold the car to another dealer, and it had since been resold to a retail purchaser!

When it came time to trade back, the dealer offered the customer $4,000.00 for his car, which the customer knew was the ACV, because the dealer showed him he was faking the figures to the bank!

Even so, the customer upon hiring an attorney was paid $8,000.00 for his trade-in because the dealer failed to return it to him, and that was the trade-in value *on the contract*. Lawyers have made their clients a lot of money on these phony trade allowances over the years.

Another customer just refused any settlement and took the dealer to court. The judge ruled that because the finance contract the customer signed was essentially between buyer and seller (dealer) until the dealer could sell it to a bank, and since no bank had accepted it, the dealer was obligated to carry the contract himself; the dealer had no choice. The customer therefore made his payments directly to the dealer. Talk about a cash flow killer for the dealer, and a great deal for the customer, because otherwise he wouldn't have been able to finance at all!

In a large number of agreements between dealers and lenders, dealers are able to guarantee performance of the contract. Say the dealer is making a huge profit on the sale, but the bank won't finance the amount the dealer needs because it is excessive. The dealer doesn't want to lose all of this gravy, so he will sign to partially guarantee the customers payments. Maybe for the first year, the dealer stands behind the payments. If the customer fails to pay, the dealer will. His odds are good, because even if he has to make some payment or buy back a repossession, he can resell the vehicle and the only thing he loses is just part of his profit. The customers of course, are unaware of these dealer guarantees. This guarantee from a dealer is called recourse.

Some dealers do such a volume of business in this manner that they are constantly buying back repossessions. In fact, I've seen some dealers take more than 250 cars back in a single month, and pay off the balances to the lenders, and never miss a beat!

If a dealer is financially stable, the bank runs little risk with these guaranteed loans. What this type of operation does though is hurt a lot of people. The buyers who procure credit under a plan such as this, pay enormous profits to the dealers and banks involved.

These are the same customers who also roll over and end up with service contracts, paint sealants and protection packages, etch, and all of the extra profit making items dealers can think of. Even the worthless ignition-kill items that supposedly make it harder for a thief to start your car by having to insert a chip in a slot before it will start, or wave a wand, or touch a secret button. All of these items are thrust upon the unwary. Buyer beware!

We touched on the service contract, and I want to discuss it and other scams more at this time to further emphasize the dangers. Customers are often told that banks give you a better rate if you purchase credit insurance because the lender feels more secure if you have a *protected payment*. This is a lie! Period. Also, many customers are duped into believing that the lender wants the dealer to sell you a service contract so if you have a mechanical problem with the vehicle, you won't have to come up with the cost of repair and possibly affect your ability to make your monthly payment on time. This might make sense if it weren't such a crock. Don't you believe any song and dance like this for a moment! The lender couldn't care less. They base your credit approval on your credit record and your ability to pay and have no concern about any such additional profit-making schemes the dealer may be trying.

Now let's look at the finance contract itself. Remember the difference between front-end and back-end profit? Let's now put this in perspective when it comes to putting the numbers onto a bank finance contract.

The most common reference that we have in the business is that *line 3* on most finance documents is the amount of *front-end* we are financing. *Line 5* is the total of *front and back-end* money combined to equal the *total amount financed*. Let's break this down. Line 3 includes the vehicle being purchased plus any extra items such as pickup truck shells, bed liners, running boards, to name just a few. You can call these hard adds. The back-end items are such products as service contracts, paint sealants, etch schemes, credit insurance, alarms, ignition kill gimmicks, etc., we can refer to these as soft adds.

Now, with most lenders, financing approval is made with line 3 requirements having to be met. Let's say, line 3 (amount financed) must be at 100% of the MSRP (manufacturers' suggested retail price) for customers with an average credit score. This means that the lender's requirement is that for this particular individual, on a new vehicle purchase, that the most they will finance is the vehicle's list price. So after trade-in payoff on the trade and cash down, the balance to finance can't exceed the MSRP. Lenders set percentages of cost or list prices primarily based on an individual's credit score.

On a used vehicle, a lender may require the amount financed not to exceed the retail blue book on whatever guide they require to be used. Therefore, if the particular customer meets the credit criteria, the necessary debt to income ratio and whatever other stipulations, then he or she may finance at the maximum amount specified.

That sets the requirement to get to line 3. Now is when we have to look at how the back-end fits into the equation. Back-end items such as service contracts and credit life and disability insurance are most always accepted by a lender as additional amounts that they will finance over and above the requirement for line 3. It is assumed that as long as your numbers on line 3 are met, that the dealer can add service contracts and insurance to the finance document without needing the lenders permission. The only exception could be if that by adding these extras it would increase the buyer's monthly payment to one that would be in excess of what the customer could qualify for. This is all part of the eligibility requirements of the lender, i.e.; payment must not exceed 15 percent of buyer's gross monthly income. Therefore, providing the additions do not affect a loan approval, they can be added to the loan.

Now let's talk about the hard and soft adds. A hard add on the back-end is an item such as paint sealant, alarm systems, glass etching, ignition block systems, maintenance plans, and roadside assistance plans. When the dealer or finance manager sells a customer a hard add it must be able to be included on line 3 without being over the guideline requirements, so if you agree to an item that brings the balance over the limit, they will need to push you for more money down!

A soft add is generally the credit life and disability insurance, and the service contract. The lender allows soft add products because in the event they end up with a repossession, these insurance items can be cancelled with the insurance carrier, and the lender will receive the remaining unearned premium to help offset their loss.

Occasionally, you will find certain lenders that have exceptionally large volume dealers that they will allow to consider these normal hard adds to be considered able to be financed as soft adds. This increases the dealer's profit potential, as it's certainly easier to sell items if you don't have to worry about keeping the dollars financed under any restrictions. Your only limitation is how much payment the customer can stand!

In a lot of sales, the customer is willing to pay most any payment necessary just to make the purchase, but the dealer is limited to line 3 on the finance contract.

Here's an example: Let's say that the lender will finance a maximum (based on a high credit score) of 110% of MSRP (Manufacturers' suggested retail price). The vehicle the customer is purchasing has an MSRP of $30,000.00. This means the maximum the lender will finance on line 3 is 110% X $30,000.00 = $33,000.00. The dealer invoice on this vehicle is $26,400.00. Now, this customer has a trade-in that has an actual cash value (wholesale) of $10,000.00 but he owes $18,000.00 on it. In auto parlance; *he's buried*! This customer has to put $1,000.00 cash down to make this work.

Here's the way they look at it: If they are to make any profit, they must sell their vehicle for $26,400.00 plus a profit of whatever they can accept over this invoice (cost) figure. They have a trade-in worth $10,000.00, but they have to pay $18,000.00 to get the title from the customer's lender. Therefore, they must add this $8,000.00 negative to their cost of $26,400.00 which equals $34,400.00. The customer has $1,000.00 to put down which leaves them a balance of $33,400.00.

Since the lender will finance a maximum of $33,000.00, it means that just to break even and make zero profit, they need another $400.00 in down payment from the customer. Let's say he can't come up with any additional down payment, the trade-in is not worth any more money, and the lender absolutely won't flex on the line 3. Now if they accept this deal, they will show a loss on the sale, except they will still receive the holdback from the factory. In a case like this, if they can sell the customer a service contract for $1,200.00 and their cost is $700.00, they can now turn this into a profit of $100.00 and still receive all of their holdback from the manufacturer.

So you see how line 3 can really hamper them and force a dealer to push really hard for the soft adds. Now in cases where the lender allows a dealer to include the previously mentioned items, such as; alarms, roadside assistance, etch, ignition blocks, maintenance contracts, etc., and instead of treating them as hard adds thus making it necessary to add them to line 3, the lender allows them as soft adds. Now they have a greater selection of profit makers that they can sell the customer without having to stay in line with any number. They appear instead as a total on line 5 of the finance document.

Here is where another twist on ethics comes into play. Take our previous example: They could have lived with the front-end loss of $400.00 and depended on the remainder of the holdback if they had to. Besides, they would still be able to sell the trade-in and make another profit on it. During the negotiation with the customer, they naturally keep the disclosure to a minimum. They don't discuss interest rates, term of the loan, and so forth if they can get away with it.

Using our example, this customer is in a position where he wants to purchase but can't come up with any more down payment. He will, however, in most of these cases, be willing to make a much higher monthly payment in order to own the new vehicle. They *could* just shake his hand and agree to the deal and take a chance that he may buy some back-end. But why should they take that chance? Instead, they'll turn it into a game of deception. In this case the dealer will explain briefly what a line 3 requirement is and how at what the lender requires for the amount to finance, and it's all because the customer owes too much on his trade, the dealer would lose too much money so it couldn't be done (lie)! "However," they explain, "this is how we can do it and you get all kinds of benefits." Then the dealer explains what extras are going to be necessary so that the small amount of profit the dealer makes on these items the customer ends up with will enable the dealer to break even. This type of buyer is really easy to pull these things on, as if he wasn't a car nut, he wouldn't be so buried in the first place!

As I mentioned earlier, the dealer could just accept the deal as it stood and take a chance on selling extras, but a dealer does so much better by forcing the sale of back-end items. This creative approach to back-end sales is not just used when close to marginal profit, but whenever it will make selling the extra products easier. It also comes in handy for just adding to an already large profit to make it larger!

Now, let's talk for a bit about down payment on your purchase. I will state up front that if you can't pay the down payment in its entirety at the time of the sale, stop and reconsider what you're doing. Dealers are notorious for taking your check now and holding it for a time in the future for your convenience. Actually, to your detriment!

There are a lot of sayings in the car business and one of them is, *cash is profit*. In the majority of car sales, the more money you have in down payment, the more profit they can make on the sale.

If a customer can put more money down, then it's easier to get him financed. A dealer can have an easier time hitting the customers' desired monthly payment, and can offer him less for trade-in. Dealers will grab all the money upfront, and then hold checks for additional down payment money for a month or more into the future. In so many cases, they are limited in the amount of profit they are able to make by the amount a lender will finance. So every additional hundred dollars he can get you to put down up-front will turn into another $100.00 of pure profit.

Take the case of the customer who is willing to buy the vehicle and doesn't even ask for a discount. He doesn't care what the price is; he's just wants to take it home. The only thing that limits a dealer's profit on this customer is the amount a lender will finance. If they are selling a vehicle that they can finance a balance of $20,000.00 on, and the customer has $4,000.00 cash down, they can charge $24,000.00 for the vehicle. However, if they can hold another check for $2,000.00 to be cashed next month, they pick up another $2,000.00 in profit by charging $26,000.00 for the vehicle. Conversely, if they own a car for $18,000.00 and a lender will finance $20,000.00 and a customer offers them $26,000.00 for it, they'd better be able to get him to put $6,000.00 cash down. If he can't, and can only put down $1,000.00, they must sell the car for $21,000.00 so they can take his $1,000.00 and discount the price to him. That's the hard part, giving the discount when the customer doesn't care or hasn't asked for it, or, if he has, but loves the car enough you can hold the full price! Yes, there are enough people that are that easy! Oh yes, prices can and do fluctuate like this based on what they can get! Oftentimes it is made easy for them by the true payment buyer. This customer really doesn't care how the numbers look, as long as the payment is where he can handle it.

Dealers take checks for down payment in many ways. Most of the time, you must have a checking account in your name. They will ask you to write checks for future down payments for as much as they can get you to agree to. Most often the first payment on your loan will start in around a month or a month and a half so it's a terrible idea for you to still be finishing making your down payment when your regular payments are following right behind. People lose all sense of reason when they want a vehicle badly enough. People who haven't saved five hundred dollars in six months suddenly feel that they can cover a check for $1,000.00 in just one month! Unfortunately, what so often happens is that these people will skip another payment on something else in order to cover the check. This just creates a worsening of the customer's financial situation and can cause untold financial woes in the future. The situation is further exacerbated by the fact that in many cases the dealer is pushing hard for this additional down payment *just to increase his gross profit*! The customer who covers his hold check by skipping some other bill may just cause himself a domino effect with his total financial obligations. All because the dealer pushed beyond reason for extra profit!

The rule here that I believe you need to hold firmly to is, "If you don't have it, don't spend it!" Period! You don't want to start out a new purchase on the wrong foot. If you don't have the money when it's time for the dealer to cash your down payment hold check, it's not just like you can call him up and ask to be forgiven the amount. Most dealers are using some form of check guarantee company, so if your check bounces, the dealer still collects his money and you're going to be responsible to an impartial third party. The check companies won't be understanding, and they will want their money, and they will garnish your wages quickly!

Don't write hold-checks. Learn to say no! It's surprising the things that happen when you halt further negotiating. You may find out that the dealer may just find a way to get by without the additional down payment! If he does, be cautious. If you find out he can suddenly dispense with the hold check, ask where it went. If five minutes before, he needed another $1,000.00 down payment and now he doesn't, what is making the difference? Has the price gone down $1,000.00? If so, has the payment also decreased? If yes to one and no to the other, why not? Did the interest rate go up to compensate for the price going down? Whenever a change occurs as you're negotiating, look for a consequence of that change. Be wary! Anytime you're told what must be done to make a sale work and you can't do it and then it works anyway, question it.

The old saying, "Don't look a gift horse in the mouth" doesn't apply here. Anytime a dealer says he can get by without what he said he needed, such as cash down, find out why! Possibly if the price goes down when you can't pay more down payment, that tells you that maybe your negotiations weren't that good to begin with. Furthermore, if the price goes down $1,000.00, you need to refer to the factor chart in this book and re-compute your monthly payment to make sure it went down accordingly!

Every move a car dealer makes has a consequence. If they save you $1,000.00 in cash down and the payment stays the same as they had previously quoted, two things jump out; either they had enough leg in the payment, so they could lose $1,000.00 and just not show you where it went, or maybe they slipped in something like a service contract, whereby he makes up his $1,000.00 in profit on it. Now, the dealer may also show you that by giving you $1,000.00 by lowering the down payment, he may need to sell you (force you to take) an accessory that he can make up the profit of $1,000.00 on. Just make certain that they can justify what they say they are doing. Anytime a car dealer puts something in your hand, he may be reaching in your pocket to get it back!

It is especially helpful for you to know where you are at any time you are negotiating a car deal. As I mentioned earlier, know what interest rate you qualify for and use your factor chart to constantly refigure your payment every time anything changes. In this manner, you will be aware of packed payments or how every change affects you. Like the customer we discussed, that could buy the next model upgrade if they knew what the actual payment was rather than being unaware of reality.

Some states are now making a packed payment unlawful. The law states that a payment stated to customer during negotiations must be an actual payment and not packed with room for the back-end profit. An example would be the customer that qualifies for a payment of $450.00 based on a seven percent interest rate and the payment is presented to the customer at $490.00. If he agreed to the $490.00 per month, the finance manager can sell quite a bit of back-end profit such as warranties, protection packages, maintenance agreements, etc. and the customer would think he's getting an incredible deal because the payment wouldn't go up. Many states are finally trying to correct this type of deceitful practice, but anything the law can address, a dealer can find a way around it. Just learn to protect yourself. There is no such thing as *truth in lending* when a car person is in control of the process.

To quote a non-packed payment, since interest isn't voluntarily disclosed during the offering and negotiating stage, it's easy for the dealer to calculate the payment at a fifteen percent rate rather than the seven percent you qualify for, and adding extra. This is why you must be constantly aware of what numbers are being used and calculate your own payment as you go. Using this example, by figuring a higher rate, the dealer skirts the law and still has a packed payment. He cannot get away with this if you are continually calculating your own payment.

When skirting around the interest rate disclosure, a dealer may be evasive when you try to pin down the APR. When you ask what interest rate they are basing their calculations on, they can come back at you by stating that they cannot quote you an exact rate until they run a credit check. That's true, but they can figure it at a rate they don't promise you. NO! Don't ever let them run your credit until you have shaken hands on a deal! You should already know what rate you can get, and need to be using it and doing your own calculations! Let the dealer show you whatever he wishes on payments. You are to work only on the price, trade, cash down, and compute your own payments.

When you go car shopping, you had better know your credit score and the interest rate you qualify for so do not ever let anyone run your credit until you have finished all negotiating. I'll give you another true story of just one time I saw this happen.

After a long time negotiating, the customers changed their minds, got mad and left. The sales manager got really belligerent and ran their credit check 19 more times in three days. Why? Quite often when someone is out trying to make multiple purchases, or having a flood of credit inquiries, the credit reporting agencies' computers send up a warning flag! Not only did that happen, but those people couldn't purchase anything for over a week, and their credit score dropped significantly, due to all the inquiries!

Just a note here about interest rates. Sometimes a dealers' source of financing may have a better rate than you can get through your own source. Always compare with what you know you can get. The auto manufacturer may offer special financing rates. Be cautious however, because if you have the choice of receiving a rebate, or a special financing rate, I would always take the rebate! Why? First of all, the manufacturer is making a sale gamble that 90% of the people who opt for the interest rate will likely trade the vehicle before they are very far into the contract, so they aren't exposed to a no-profit loan for all that long. You ask why? Because the lure of a zero percent, or low percentage rate loan is a good hook, but it will be at a shorter term, and buyers may soon find themselves strapped, and end up re-financing at their own bank to get their payment down to a manageable level. Also, these special plans are put in place to help sell slow moving or less popular vehicles! Surprised? Why would they incentivize a product that sells well? When you take the rebate, you have the money up front!

By offering a special rate, they sell unpopular cars, and the buyers of these vehicles soon see why there was a special incentive, find that they aren't happy with it, and trade it rather quickly. Maybe within a year? Advantage — manufacturer! You pay off the contract and the special rate is over!

In addition, if you have an accident and the car is totaled, the manufacturer will not allow your insurance company to replace the vehicle on the finance contract. No, it is cancelled, and you must finance elsewhere, and you just lost your special rate!

Always take the rebate if one if offered, and finance the lower balance through your own lender!

PRACTICE. Be your own finance manager. The Finance chapter is where you win, lose or draw!

I'd like for you now to do some practice, until you feel comfortable. We'll run through a few scenarios, and I'll show you how to calculate your own payments on the spot. Your relationship with the dealers' personnel will now be one where you gain their respect, and keep you in absolute control of the process.

Grab a calculator, some scratch paper, and you and your significant other spend the time to both work on practicing the methods that will hopefully change your standard of living! If you're alone, then sit beside yourself and do it.

PRACTICE BEING YOUR OWN FINANCE MANAGER.

Let's run through a couple of calculations. We'll say that the vehicle you've negotiated a deal on, after trade in, leaves a balance to finance of $28,000.00. You know that you are able to secure financing at 6% interest.

Using the factor chart (there's an extra one in the back of the book you can tear out) we look at 6%, and going across to the 60 months column, gives us a multiplier of .01933.

Next we multiply .01933 times the $28,000.00, and our payment will be $541.24. This amount may be slightly different than what the dealer quotes, because they usually slip in *45 days until first payment*. This delays your payment for a month and a half, and some people like that. I don't, because I'm paying for 15 days extra interest for five years. This factor is based on first payment due in 30 days.

Now, if you don't feel comfortable at this payment, you can either stretch out the term, or put more cash down.

Looking at 72 months at 6%, our factor is .01657. Multiply times our $28,000.00, and we have a payment of $463.96.

You can see that if your payment goal is $500.00, that a 66 month term might be your answer, as the payment will actually be $499.00 and change.

Once you have been pre-qualified by your lender, ask them to run a series of factors for you if your rate or term desired is not on this chart, or you can do this on your computer at home.

For example; enter $1,000.00 balance, 54 months for the term, and 6.25% interest. The payment comes out a $21.29 per month for every $1,000.00 borrowed at $6\frac{1}{4}$%, for four and $\frac{1}{2}$ years. Your new factor is .02129. You can see that if you wanted to finance your $28,000.00 for just $4\frac{1}{2}$ years at this 6.25% rate, your payment would be $596.00.

Once you have a set of factors, when you go vehicle shopping, you will have with you, multipliers for all terms available to you, and with a three dollar calculator, you can instantly see your own payment. Now, your thoughts and conversation with your partner can be kept to a silent sharing of your calculator screen, and the dealer may not have a clue as to what you're looking at.

They won't have an idea as to what your finances are, the payment you're considering, or how much more they have to cave in to hit the magic number to earn your business. Everyone you come in contact with in a dealership is always trying to get inside your head! This keeps them out!

They are looking for what makes you tick, and how to *close* you. You must keep your desires and thoughts confidential, because you are going to stay in control of this buying process. Yes, it is perfectly acceptable to be secretive and polite at the same time. We car people really don't mind.

I have used vehicle financing terms as long as 8 years, and I'd bet that the folks that signed up for that long a term would trade again in less than four years. Talk about buried!

I will mention here that one cannot always blame the dealer for this craziness. I've had customers come in who regularly finance at these long terms, because through the process of several trades, this is their last resort! Once they can no longer handle the payment at the longest term, and can't put enough additional cash down to get approved, they are most often just one step away from bankruptcy!

So many people are conned into taking out or adding to a home equity loan to buy a vehicle! Over the years, I have seen countless occasions where the car is carried right along with the home, on a thirty year term. Please do not do this!

It surely makes negotiating payments easier, and the payoff on the trade-in is not so important, or easy to determine, because it's usually lumped in with other purchases. The only thing a dealer has to do is obtain a check from the customer's bank for the additional monies he needs and the title to the trade. Banks are like any other lender. They are there to service their customers, and to loan money. A loan officer is not likely going to advise a customer on what to do, as long as they are able to safely handle the loan.

Another way the factor can be of benefit is when you first begin your process of buying a new vehicle. Get an idea as to how much your automobile insurance will increase for the added (retail) value of the new vehicle. I say retail price, because you will want *replacement value* coverage. Figure to pay the sales tax out of pocket (you're crazy if you finance the tax over the whole term).

Now, let's say your budget can comfortably afford a new payment of $450.00 per month. You need now to determine how long before you decide to trade again, and try to hold down the length of your finance term as short as you can.

Let's say you feel safe with a monthly payment of $450.00, and are comfortable financing for five years, and you qualify for a 5% loan — Divide $450.00 (desired payment), by the 5% factor for 60 months, which is .01887. The answer is $23,847.37. This means that after you trade in or sell your present car, pay whatever down payment you plan, and all fees are paid (also never finance a year of two license for five years) that you can finance just under $24,000.00. If you don't plan to put any additional cash down, except tax and fees, the difference the dealer needs had better be at this $24,000.00, right?

Now what happens if you owe $4,000.00 more on your trade than it's worth? Here are your options:

Pay an extra $4,000.00 cash out of pocket (the best).

Accept the higher payment, based on the amount to finance of $28,000.00 ($24,000.00 + negative equity of $4,000.00) if your credit will allow it; which will be a new payment of $528.00.

Stretch the term (if again, your credit qualifies you to do so), if you are still trying to hit the $450.00 per month. Looking at a six year term, you see that taking a balance of $28,000.00 times the 72 month factor of .01611, your payment will be $451.00.

Many banks charge higher rates for longer terms, so ask these questions when your banker is calculating your factors ahead of time. So, you see in this case, you will be able to make the payment work by stretching the loan term for an additional year.

The downside is going a year longer than you were comfortable in doing, which maybe isn't so bad, but don't forget, you're also carrying $4,000.00 in negative equity from your trade-in. That's an additional six years to finish paying off your last vehicle, plus the depreciation on the new one!

So many cases I've seen with long term finance contracts and short term trading cycles; people are still paying for cars they bought 10 or 12 years before! This is the life of the typical payment buyer, and a great percentage of Americans go through their entire lives in this upside down position. This is what I hope this book will help change.

Now, if you forgot to get the factors, or are caught on a sudden impulse stop; which happens to all of us, do like I've always done. I carry the formula we discussed on page 76 written on a card in my wallet.

$$\$ \text{ X } \% \div 365 \text{ X } 17 \text{ X M} + \$ \div M$$

It looks long, but takes only a minute. Let's use our example, and do a continuous calculation.

Substitute: $ = amount financed ($28,000.00).

Enter 28000 X (times) .05 (%), ÷ (divide by) 365, X (times) 17, X (times) 72 (months financed), + (plus) 28000, ÷ (divide by) 72 (months financed). Your payment comes out at $454.09. Practice doing this and you can use any price, rate, and term; and do it all in less than a minute. I carry a calculator the size of a business card, and I have this formula written in permanent ink on the front of it.

Never go to a car dealership without it. You can always borrow the salesman's calculator, but he won't know this formula. I guarantee it! Maybe one in 5,000 car people have heard of it, but I doubt the number is even that high.

Let's do another one:

$30,000.00 to finance, 72 months, six percent interest.

$ (30000) X % (.06) ÷ (365) X (17) X months (72) + $ (30000) ÷ months (72); your payment is approximately $500.00, a little slower than $30,000 X factor of .01657, which is an accurate payment of $497.00, but it is so close, and if the dealer starts quoting percentages to you, or offering interest rates in lieu of discounts, you can quickly compare to see if it is a good deal for you.

This is the point in your life where you can begin to turn things around. Take control of your negotiations and your emotions.

If you have difficulty in openly calculating in front of your salesperson and the manager, just ask for a few minutes of privacy, a pen, paper, calculator, or anything else you may need.

The dealers' people will be more than happy to accommodate you. I always loved it when people asked for this privacy; I knew that we were at the point where they were trying to make the deal work, and were preparing to make me a counter offer. When you ask for privacy, they will most likely offer to get you some more refreshment;

go for it, you're going to make a deal!

Take your time, calculate your scenarios, and if you have any interim questions, wave them over; they'll be watching, and ready to help. This is where you gain tons of respect, and it becomes a win, win situation.

Now, when you make a counter offer, you can tailor it to your exact needs, and you don't have to wonder what the new payment would be if they only meet you half way on the price or trade.

Either calculate it in front of them, or ask for more time. This is a big decision for you, and you're going to live with it for years, and we car people are affected only for a short time. So you can see, we understand.

Just a note here to show the value of having factors available; one evening during a big sale, and with a showroom full of buyers, a car accident blew our transformer and our power went out! I sent a salesperson down the street to a store that had power, and he bought all the candles he could find. We set them on our sales desks, and with a factor chart on the sales office desk, and pocket calculators, we sold ten vehicles! We wrote the contracts by hand, and had a successful evening!

CHAPTER 7
EXTENDED WARRANTY? — OR THE SERVICE CONTRACT SCAM

There is a relatively more modern type of service contract (extended warranty) that dealers have been pushing for years now. Whenever a customer doesn't wish to purchase a service contract it's because he sees no value in the product or doesn't want the extra cost. He may have purchased them in the past and either didn't use it or it may not have covered the problem that occurred, or other complications. Also, he may have read my original book, "The Underground Blue Book!"

Now, the dealer can offer you a service contract that if you don't use it, you get all but fifty dollars back, of the original amount. Sounds good doesn't it? On the surface! But let's examine this further. Let's say you go for the program and purchase the coverage to extend your protection up to six years and 75,000 miles of warranty coverage. The dealer charges you $3,000.00 for this policy, but you aren't concerned with the cost as you otherwise might be because you know that at the end of the term you will get $2,950.00 coming back to you!

Now, let's look at the reality of this scenario. Look closely at your money-back agreement. It states that if you have not used the coverage, you receive all but $50.00 back. The fine print in this one is that you must go to the end of the policy period and not have used it! This means that you must keep this vehicle for six years or 75,000 miles of usage! What are the chances of you doing this? Very slim if you're like the majority of the car buying public. If you trade early, you will receive only a *standard cancellation* of this service contract and therefore, you've paid extra money (these policies cost more than standard extended contracts) and received no benefit from this expensive promise.

Suppose now that you are an exception and you are nearing the end of your service contract period and you still have the vehicle. Say you have two years to go and 24,000 miles remaining when you have a problem with the vehicle. Your factory warranty has expired and the repair bill is $500.00. You now ask yourself, do I claim it under the service contract, in which case I lose my $2,950.00 after the next two years are up? What happens though, if you pay this repair out of pocket and then before the policy period ends you have another breakdown? You see, the insurance company has a pretty safe bet either way you go. They're counting on the fact that most people will trade long before the policy is fully used, and also that buyers will be reluctant to use the policy on smaller claims! You also cannot go back to collect the $500.00 after the fact should you have no further problems until the end of the contract period!

I cannot repeat often enough how cautious you must be throughout the entire car-buying process. You may do everything right during the negotiating process and then roll right over and buy some stupid product that you pay way too much for and will never use.

Now let's look further into the world of service contracts. As the finance manager goes through your title work *casually*, the conversation will soon get around to how you are paying for the vehicle, down payments, monthly payments, and if you are letting the dealership arrange the financing will be covered. They will, of course, try to get you to finance through the dealers' bank.

The conversation will lead to whether or not you have an extended warranty on your trade-in vehicle that they can *help you cancel*. (A trial run to see if you are the type of person who buys extended warranties.) If you bought one before, you are more likely to buy again and the price and payments will now be presented to include an extended warranty on your new purchase (Assumptive close). This is especially easy if you are a payment buyer. Everything will be quoted to you in terms of how much a month it will change and price will seldom even be discussed. Remember, *A payment buyer is God's gift to car dealers.*

Don't forget, the business or finance manager is another salesperson. They get paid only if you buy something from them. If you hold fast and refuse all of their offers for extras, their mood will change and you will be processed very quickly and cooly because you just ruined their percentages that help them earn bonuses! Don't get me wrong, they will likely not turn rude, but this is their livelihood; you don't buy, they don't eat! Not to be concerned, they'll more than make it up on the next guy!

So you wonder why dealers don't just hire salaried title clerks? Because every department is an income producing entity except the true business office, and *everybody* else sells, or attempts to sell something.

Now, on to the extended warranty, or more appropriately called the service contract. This is sold *hard and heavy.* I have never seen so many people purchase a product that they will not ever use! People buy extended service contracts because of a fear of loss, although with the vast majority, they could never use the coverage!

Reason being; they trade vehicles too often. A lot of people trade vehicles regularly where they are still covered by the manufacturer's warranty. They are easily convinced, for they are obviously very conservative and security conscious folks to begin with and the possibility of keeping the new vehicle longer than the previous ones is the lure. Combine that with the refund of the unused portion of the standard service contract, and the hook is easily set again! The unused portion of the service contract doesn't amount to more than a few dollars because even though the vehicle has continually been covered by the factory warranty, the service contract premium starts being earned and used up starting from day one! That's right; your service contract premium is being earned even before it ever goes into effect.

I have met so many thousands of buyers who always think, "This time it's going to be different!" They feel that all of their prior purchases have been wrong and this is finally the right one for them. Because of this type of thinking, the car person can play on this and inject the positive *buy it all because this one you're going to keep forever* philosophy.

The greater majority of people do not do anything different now than they ever did, however, and all this great thinking will be soon forgotten as people rarely change their established patterns, as they've grown accustomed to this pattern, and in a couple of years they'll go through the same procedure again and pay for another service contract they won't use.

PAY CLOSE ATTENTION HERE: The other factor that many car buyers think is an important factor is that the trade-in will be worth more if it has a service contract with it. Wrong! If it is transferable at all, it is only transferable to the second owner. If you trade the vehicle to a dealer, then he becomes the second owner, voiding the warranty when he resells the car again. Besides, a trade-in with a service contract is *undesirable* to a dealer. You may think he could sell it for more money with the contract, but he couldn't and wouldn't. He will sell his own warranty, and if he finances the vehicle, he will add in the price of the service contract, thus raising the amount to be financed, and he will earn finance profit on the increased contract amount also. Plus he will make a large profit on the sale of this contract, so yours is unneeded and unnecessary for anyone! The salesman will push you on the increased trade-in value, but it's a lie; a bold lie!

Most service contracts are never used and a great percentage are forgotten about when the customer trades vehicles. The service contract company benefits because they keep all the premium and have no repairs to pay for, and the dealer is happy because he has no charge backs for cancellation. So, the only loser is the poor customer who bought the package and maybe, depending on how straightforward the dealership was, didn't even know it was included in their financing.

Some of you are wondering how people could be slickered into buying service contracts under these scenarios, but when everything is all excitement and glitter and the buyer is made to feel like a very special person, guards are let down and they end up partying in shark filled waters.

Here are some more fraudulent pitches that you never see in writing! Let's discuss now, the sales pitches used to discredit the manufacturers' warranties. Correct! There are training programs conducted by the companies that sell service contracts that are designed to train the dealers' finance manager to trick the buyer into believing that the new vehicle warranty is not adequate. This training is conducted on a, "You didn't hear this from me" basis by the instructors. Some of their *off the record training* is directed toward playing with the wording of the factory coverage. Such as, "Your manufacturers' obligation is to provide you with a vehicle free of defects in material and workmanship." This, or something like it, is printed in most statements of warranty coverage. The finance manager will read this to you verbatim and then, look you in the eye and say, "But not free of failures!"

The pitch training continues: "There are three primary reasons why a manufacturer can deny a claim." "The first one is climate. I'll give you an example, take the state of Washington. They use their windshield wipers four times more than in any other part of the country. In Arizona, it's air conditioning that's used all the time. Both of these problems could be denied, because of excessive use over and above the norm. The norm being the average across the U.S.A."

"The second reason a manufacturer can deny a claim is road conditions. If you're going down the road and you splash water up on a computer condenser and it shorts out, it's not covered. Now if it was a defective part or if it was installed wrong, then it's covered, but what are the odds of that?"

"The third and most common reason for which all manufacturers deny claims is personal driving habits. Otherwise known as wear and tear!" These pitches to discredit and minimize the value of your factory warranty go on and on!

This is just a small sampling of the extensive training, all designed to portray the factory warranty as inadequate and of little value. Can you believe this can of bull? This is what people are being hammered with to scare them about the very product the dealer is selling and should be happily bragging about! You're told up front how great it is, and then some whore in the finance department tells you what a crummy warranty you're getting! Excuse my language, but the factory should send out secret shoppers to catch these crooks! Then you realize that maybe the factory doesn't care as long as it sells cars!

Let's continue with the scare tactics training program: The finance manager is trained to disparage the factory warranty by homing in on the *limited aspect* and to create doubt on whether or not the manufacturer can be counted on to take care of you. They stress the fact that tires and batteries are not covered (they are covered, naturally, by the company that made them).

How's this for a pitch, "Amazing a ten billion dollar company can't provide a rental car for vehicles broken down in my service department. They used to provide rental cars, the reason they don't is cost. The higher the price of the vehicle, the more the limitation of the warranty." I'll bet the manufacturers would really be proud to hear this line of bull. This and the others are verbatim sales pitches.

So this gives you a small part of just one scenario that is taught to the finance managers in order to break down your resistance to their pitch. When you enter the realm of the finance manager, you have to remember, you're up against a professional. Unfortunately, the ethics mostly evaporated from the car business years ago, and now you have to be continually on guard.

Remember this, the people who sell these service contracts are all *commissioned sales people*, from the after-market reps and trainers to the finance manager in the dealership, they are all paid on how much they sell!

When huge profits are at stake, very high priced trainers are employed to train very high priced finance managers. To earn incomes in the fifteen to thirty thousand dollar monthly figures, these people are very good at what they do. While you're sitting, trying to justify another $10.00 dollars in payment, the finance manager you're working with may be earning that $30,000.00 per month!

So far I have been speaking of service contracts sold unnecessarily on new vehicles. Used vehicles on the other hand, are a different story. Just analyze carefully what you get for how much, because I still feel that used car service contracts are also a scam!

I, of course, advise you to have your mechanic thoroughly examine the vehicle before you buy it. Don't forgo the mechanical inspection because the seller throws in a house warranty for maybe 30 to 90 days. This may be done to make you feel secure about their integrity, but may be given just to stop you from having the vehicle checked out by a qualified mechanic.

The easiest way to promote trust and stop someone from further inspecting what you're selling is to guarantee it. Many used cars are sold with the dealer giving an *in-house warranty*. Something that makes a customer feel good without going through the costs of paying an outside mechanic to check out the vehicle before they buy. People feel the dealer must be selling a good product because he's standing behind it. Yes, but how far behind it? Don't bite on it! Take it to a mechanic, and pay the money to check it out. You'll never regret it!

Let's say you agree to buy the car as is, and after the free 90 day warranty runs out, the engine blows, or the transmission breaks down. Flaws that maybe could have been caught by an inspection up front and that were bound to go bad over time. Always inspect what you expect!

Don't forget that prices of used vehicle service contracts are always negotiable and watch for deductibles and limitations on occurrences and claim maximums.

Whatever you're being asked to buy rates a thorough inspection, and if you don't understand, ask questions until you do. Once you sign the papers, it's like giving birth to a two-headed baby; you'd better take it home and learn to love it, because it's all yours.

The country is full of professional finance manager training schools. There are throngs of trainers who come at a high price and who do nothing but train people full time, just to sell you products!

Finance managers spend years honing their skills through special training and experimentation on people such as you. Do you really think you are going to match wits with someone who trains every day for something you do once every few years? Of course, what they say makes sense! It's well-rehearsed to sound great!

When you're playing in my ball park, you'd better bring your own ball, and your own umpire! I promise you, my bases are always loaded! By the way, did I mention; don't buy service contracts!

Now before a lot of people start tying nooses in their ropes, remember that good selling does not have to be dishonest. If they sell you a product by being forceful and disarming, as long as they haven't lied; is it wrong? Look closely for the small scar on the rear of the finance manager's head. It was from the conscience-removal operation.

I just remind the reader that there are a lot of people out there who, for lack of sales ability, must resort to lying and cheating. That happens in all walks of life and because some do wrong, all should not be condemned. Just always realize that people like me who close as many as twenty sales per day get a lot of practice. How much do you get?

Selling, closing, and financing cars is a professional occupation that if you're good, pays very well. Just watch out for the untrustworthy. When you see the truth leave the negotiating table, get up and leave. When they start to lie, it can only get worse. Put them on notice, and don't put up with falsehoods!

A good, strong sales pitch is to be appreciated. I don't mind it at all. I can respect someone who believes in their product and appreciate a strong sales pitch, but when someone finds it necessary to lie to me, the trust is gone and so am I. This should be your guide. They make their living by selling, and I would hope you would give them a chance to present their wares. Then decide if you want it or not.

Now let's take a look at another scam — selling service contracts on leases! No one can ever make me believe that selling someone a service contract on a new car lease is doing anything other than stealing! Flat-out stealing!

A person who leases a vehicle is not concerned with owning the vehicle after the lease period is up -- at least they had better not be! You lease a vehicle to use it for a given number of months and then turn it in! Period!

I'll get into leasing in another chapter, but leasing and then purchasing the vehicle when the lease is up is dumb! Yes, dumb! Yet a lot of salesmen try to convince you that, "You will probably buy the vehicle at the end of the lease," so you need to buy the extras such as paint sealants, fabric protectants, and everything else they can throw at you because you're leasing now, but with eventual ownership in mind. Bull! Absolute hogwash! Buying extras on leases is stupid!

Now the finance manager takes a run at you to purchase an extended warranty because, "Knowing you will certainly purchase this vehicle after the lease is up," you will want the extended coverage. Again, bull! If you wanted a used car, you'd be buying one now! Don't buy a service contract on a lease! Never! NEVER, NEVER!

You know, the whole gist of this service contract pitch when you buy a new vehicle is so you have coverage when the factory warranty runs out. So you finance it in with the car, pay interest on it throughout the period of the loan, and likely never use it. What a waste!

If you really would like to have a longer warranty, then here's your solution: You needn't worry about buying an extended factory warranty later on. When you buy a new vehicle, the manufacturer keeps track of the mileage reported when you visit the dealership for warranty work and the scheduled intervals required to keep your manufacturers' warranty coverage in effect. They know based on your driving habits about how many miles a month you are putting on the vehicle.

Long before your factory warranty is up, either mileage or time wise, you will begin receiving solicitations *from the manufacturer* to buy an extended factory warranty. That's right, instead of International Gotcha' Warranty Corp., you will be able to purchase an extended warranty directly from the company that built your vehicle. They will even offer you payment plans, without interest charges!

So, you see how foolish it is to buy a service contract on a new vehicle that you may never use, pay a higher monthly payment, pay interest on the premium and do all of this far in advance of ever having a need for it. Even if they try to convince you to buy the manufacturers' extended warranty instead of some Mickey Mouse plan, don't buy it up front, ever! You don't need it now, you don't want it now!

Another statistic that may interest you is that 85% of all extended warranties go unused when purchased on new vehicles at the time of purchase. Now let's look at another scenario: What happens if you buy the contract and while you are still under factory warranty, you wreck the vehicle? Now you really lose! Yes, you can receive a short-rate cancellation of the unused premium (if you remember). It will be a greatly reduced amount from what you initially paid for the policy even though it was useless because you were still covered by the manufacturers' warranty. It's like buying an extra engine to store in your garage in case someday you'll need it. Then the car gets totaled, and the engine is never needed. In the turmoil after an accident, people seldom remember about cancelling the service contract and then they lose it all!

Let's say you trade in this vehicle while you still owe money on it. You cannot use the cancellation of the service contract policy as a down payment on your next vehicle unless you buy again from the same dealer, and he sells you another service contract. Why? Because an outright service contract cancellation must be done through the dealership you bought it from. If you buy again from the dame dealer, they can do the cancellation and allow you the refund on the spot, but if you buy from anyone else, your original dealer will take around two months to send your cancellation in on their regular monthly report and usually these cancellations have to go through channels back to the service contract company. Since you now bought from someone else, the original selling dealer has no reason to rush things. He may purposely delay longer in hopes you forget about it and just go away.

So now, when trading, you are burdened by having an even higher loan balance on your new purchase because your loan payoff includes this old service contract. Sure, you may eventually receive your money, but that won't reduce your monthly payment to what it would have been without this carryover burden.

Another problem could occur if the dealer you bought it from is no longer in business. Maybe the dealer went under and no one took over the dealership. Most service contracts are regulated by the individual states' insurance commissioner. Now, add a trip to the state insurance department for their help in tracking down the company and securing your refund! Good luck with that one! As fast as these insurance companies go under, you are likely looking at a loss.

Let's look at an even scarier scenario. What if the dealer you bought the contract from was self-insured? That's correct — I remember not too many years back where a dealer could license his own warranty company in many states and for as small an amount as $5,000.00 in assets. This means he can sell service contracts (also the same for credit life and disability insurance) and collect the premiums and his company alone is responsible for paying claims and administering the entire program. If you have a claim, that dealer determines your eligibility. He decides your fate. After all, you're dealing with an insurance company with a whole $5,000.00 in assets!

So, back to what happens if that dealer goes out of business? Talk to the mirror, you're now S.O.L! So many things can go wrong, why be foolish with your money? People do things generally for two reasons; a hope for gain or a fear of loss! Don't let a fear of loss cause you to make a foolish and unnecessary decision.

If you are buying a used vehicle that has no manufacturers' warranty left on it, then after a mechanics' inspection, you may wish to consider buying a service contract. Also keep in mind that there are many competitive warranty companies out there — you don't have to buy from the dealer if they aren't price competitive! And, don't forget to negotiate! Everything for sale is negotiable!

I will again repeat my feelings on extended warranties (service contracts). Do not buy a service contract at the time of purchase on a new vehicle that has a manufacturers' warranty! You will have plenty of time before the standard coverage ever runs out to buy additional coverage *directly from the factory*!

With the trading cycles that most new car buyers have today, there is little likelihood that you will ever even buy one later on, because odds are, after you finish the factory warranty period, the vehicle will be broken in and any defects already repaired. How many used Toyotas and other cars are there out there with over 300,000 miles on them? Lots! Do your proper oil changes, and other maintenance and you'll probably never need a longer warranty anyway.

I have known hundreds of vehicle owners who said, "I'll just keep this car until I run it into the ground," and they're still driving them with hundreds of thousands of miles! Some over a million!

Save your money on warranties, chances are great that other than for small items, you save enough by not buying service contracts that over time, you can accumulate enough extra money to buy an entire new car with the savings! These suggestions aren't being made lightly. I have formed my negative opinions of service contracts by forty years of experience in the trenches.

To sum it all up:

> Don't buy it until you need it. (Never pay up front for a service contract on a new vehicle.)

> Never buy a service contract on a lease.

> Always purchase the warranty from the manufacturer of the vehicle (factory warranty). Once your original warranty is about to expire, and only if you're keeping the vehicle, naturally.

> Shop around for a service contract if buying a used vehicle not covered by remaining factory coverage.

> Strongly consider your need for even having a used car service contract at all!

CHAPTER 8
BUYING A USED VEHICLE

When buying a used vehicle, remember the uppermost rule; CAVEAT EMPTOR (Buyer Beware)! Once you drive away in any vehicle, you own it — period! Don't rely on any verbal promises that you've received from the dealer. What you see, you get!

Before you should even care about your newfound negotiating skills, you must make sure that you find the right vehicle. Shopping for a used vehicle is a lot more difficult than purchasing a new one. The used car may or may not have any manufacturers' warranty remaining. Let's first address this warranty:

Today, new vehicles come with varying warranties, and you must look closely as to what is covered and for how long. If you find a used vehicle you think you want to buy, call a dealer who sells the product new and ask what coverage that particular year and model came with. The dealer's service department should be readily able to provide that information. Also, when you have chosen a specific vehicle, call the service department for that make and ask them to input the individual VIN (vehicle identification number). They will be able to tell you the *in-service date* for that exact vehicle, which is the date the warranty actually started for the original owner. Also ask if the remaining warranty transfers to successive owners, as many do not!

This is extremely important when the mileage on the car is below 36,000 miles, but it's two model years old. You may feel and be told by the salesperson that you still have factory warranty coverage. By calling to find out the in-service date, you may find out that the car was sold early in the prior model year from when it was manufactured, and that the three years has long since expired, since warranties are generally time or mileage; whichever comes first.

Manufacturers introduce their new models at various times, but instead of current year nomenclature, they introduce them as advance models, such as a 2014 model introduced in Spring of 2013, a 2011 model that's actually brought out on the market in late 2009, and a 2009 model that maybe came out in 2007. How about a '12 in Spring of '11! Now I see a new arrival 2015, and we're in Summer of 2014!

Don't be overwhelmed by the sales pitch. You are the only one who can ascertain the truth and you must do this yourself. Now of course, having a remainder of factory warranty is not critical to your decision, but it could be a tremendous plus. Take the vehicle that you purchase and find out a week later that the transmission is slipping — a manufacturers' warranty may cover you. You may also find out the hard way why the previous owner traded it in!

Do you believe that if you had purchased a service contract that you would be covered in that same scenario? Wrong! Service contracts cover for mechanical breakdown. A slipping transmission is not a breakdown. You will end up paying the bill! Sure you can try to let it go until it breaks down and hope that the service contract company will pay for it, but you'll probably lose here too. They will check and find out that you previously had it diagnosed for the problem (records will be on file somewhere), and failed to have it repaired and therefore, they will turn down your claim because of improper maintenance. You won't win! Never believe that a newly purchased warranty will cover an already existing problem. Those companies aren't stupid! In this scenario, the previous owner probably had his claim rejected, and that's on file; so then he traded it in.

The majority of used cars are sold by telling the customer that they, "Don't have to worry about the condition of the car, because the dealers' mechanics would have caught anything wrong with it." They go to great lengths to convince the buyer how caring and trustworthy the dealer is, while the used car manager, on the flip side, is instructing his used car technicians to cut corners every way they can. I know how the used vehicles are checked by the used car mechanics! You had better beware!

A lot of salespeople and managers are unaware that the standard inspection policy is not anything more than hype, so even though they may be genuinely sincere in their belief in the inspection process, the burden falls on the purchaser!

Take an example of a repair needed to a used car that may take four hours, and parts cost $1,000.00. The mechanic will receive four hours of pay, and the cost of the used car will increase by four hours of wages and $1,000.00 in parts.

In this scenario, the used car manager may pay a bonus for a quick fix repair that may only last for a year, but saves the $1,000.00 in parts. You would be absolutely shocked at the cover-ups being done in these service departments, and then passing the problems on to the consumer!

Even though the dealer and everyone else in the dealership may be bragging about their reconditioned and mechanically sound used vehicles, the used car manager may have a different agenda. After all, the used car mechanics may be directly under the control of the used car manager, so they will do what he asks. If they personally get paid more for doing a partial repair, it makes them a better wage, and increases the profits of the used car department because excess repairs reflect on the judgment of the used car manager and everyone's income!

Just because a used car is said to have been reconditioned, or *factory certified*, don't believe it. I hate to sound so skeptical, but after all my years in this business, you can take what I say directly to the bank, because that's where it will pay off — in your bank account! Have it checked by your own mechanic!

Another fallacy is the one I already touched on, and that is the used car service contract. Customers are told that they really, don't have to spend the money to have the used car checked by their own mechanic — "You'll certainly want an extended warranty anyway, and anything that our mechanics may have missed would be covered." "Use the money from not doing a mechanical check to pay toward the service contract." The logic here really works well on a lot of buyers, as they probably have always rolled over for service contracts in the past!

Using the transmission as an example; any time after the purchase that you have the vehicle checked for a problem, will throw up a flag. If the car is maybe running rough, and you take it in for a check and find out you need new fuel injectors, and the cost will be $800.00, either you skip the work and suffer with it, or pay the bill. Now, it is on record that you need injectors. If you wait for it to break down (to be covered under warranty), it still won't be covered!

Again, the service contract again says; mechanical breakdown, and there is no way you can come out because deferred repairs will cause any eventual claim to be denied! I can't begin to imagine how many people have been stung on this, and most likely the salespeople were unaware that their sales pitch was false. Salespeople are continually taught to sell warranties in this manner. They receive commissions for selling them.

I do however; blame this on poor training on the dealers' part, or a purposely false training program. When management trains their people on selling techniques, they don't necessarily train them to lie. A lot of trainers deceive the sales force into *believing the pitches*. You see, even though you have confidence in the salesperson not lying to you, did someone lie to them? They may not even realize that what they are telling you is a falsehood.

Even manufacturers' warranties are *limited*. When you buy a new vehicle, they may tell you that you have bumper to bumper coverage, but you may find out that the electrical system is only covered for 12 months or 12,000 miles, whichever comes first. Batteries and tires are warranted by the manufacturer of those items and not by the company that made the vehicle. This makes sense.

So, you have selected a vehicle you want to purchase that does not have factory warranty coverage. No big deal. Now, what I recommend you do when buying any used vehicle is, arrange to take it to a mechanic, of your choice, for a complete inspection. Sure, it will cost you money, but what better security can you have? Or would you rather trust the salesperson to be honest about everything? Of course not! Most of the time the salespeople, and even the managers, have no idea where the vehicle came from, let alone its' history. Maybe it was an airport rental, or came out of a hurricane state and has flood damage! If a dealer won't allow you to take the car to your own mechanic, then walk, or better yet, run away! This is just as, or more important as seeing a CARFAX on the vehicle.

So you don't have your own mechanic? If you're buying a Toyota, take it to the service department at a Toyota dealership. You can trust the fact that any mechanic worth his salt can inspect a vehicle. Try not to use the dealer's shop that's selling the car — I've seen salespeople bribe mechanics to give a good report when this happens. Always remember; don't ask for, or expect honesty from someone who stands to benefit financially from a lie!

You may be dealing with a dealer with a great reputation, but you still need to check it out. Salespeople and managers go to great lengths to cut to the chase by trying to convince you to skip the inspection. One standard pitch is, "Our technicians are paid to find problems with our used cars. They want to do all the repairs they can find, because they make more money." Again, logical, but; not! This is a scripted lie that salespeople are led to believe! In reality, most used car mechanics are paid to short cut and jury rig everything they can, as we previously covered. A lot of them get paid on a lower rate per hour for used car checks than they do for other work, and they work on a time allowance. For example, if the technical manual allows three hours to do a job, and a technician can do it in one hour, he still gets three hours pay! Basically, although I hate to disparage everyone for the faults of some, I must! Stick to your guns!

What you need to be especially concerned with is previous collision damage, engine, drivetrain, transmission, and computer problems. Items such as power windows, power locks, etc. are minor items and can be used to negotiate the price down with the dealer, but they can also be expensive to repair and sometimes are indicative of previous accidents to the vehicle.

Many of the used cars, trucks, and SUV's out there have had a fender-bender at one time or another, and if repairs have been done properly there should be no reason not to buy them. What we really want to be wary of is frame damage! The way vehicles are built today, it is much easier to sustain frame damage in an accident than ever before.

Since so many of today's vehicles are not even built with a frame, but with *unitized construction*, it's very easy to have damage to the core support. You can also look for these things prior to making the decision to take the car to the mechanic.

Open the hood and carefully look around the inside of the engine compartment. What you're looking for are signs of chalk writing on fenders, radiator, front grille, etc. Look at the row of bolts that hold the fenders on, are they all the same? Are they all black on one side and painted the color of the vehicle on the other? Obvious damage signals! Looking behind and down under the fan, can you detect a difference in the core support bars that protrude to hold the front bumper on? Are there signs of a weld? There shouldn't be.

Next, go to the trunk. Pull back the carpet on the sides near the taillights. Are there weld and sanding signs? Next, pull up the trunk mat and look for the same signs on the trunk floor.

Now, stand back, bend down and look along the sides of the car. Are the panels all straight without ripples or waves? Do this from front to rear and rear to front on both sides. Get down eye level with the hood and the trunk and adjust your eye level to observe the plane.

Also, don't forget to open the doors and stand on the entrance so you can do the same with the roof. Stand on the rear bumper and do the same. This is especially true for sport utilities, trucks and vans. Be careful, because you don't want to wait until the first time you wash your new car to find it has a three foot long dent on the roof. I've seen brand new pickups that came from the factory with warped tops due to a weakness in the supports. Sometimes a huge dent just shows up from this fault and can't be fixed. Rather than do recalls on inferior products, the factory will punch them out and hope most purchasers will think someone did it after they bought their car. I won't mention which one, but one of the Big Three had one especially bad year where about 20 percent of their pickups had this problem! No, they didn't have a recall; they just sent them to the dealers and let them struggle to sell them!

You can also look for mismatched paint coloring when you are observing the car from different angles. Walk back and forth along the side and make certain all the paint looks the same. Paint is extremely difficult to match. Take your metallic paints for example. When coming from the factory, think of the depth you see in the metallic paint finish as an oblong diamond with the longer sides facing out toward you. This is why the finish has so much depth.

When this vehicle is repainted, the finish will still be done the best the body shop can, but now the depth of the diamond will be short-side facing out, thus cutting down on the apparent depth. They cannot do it the way the factory did. It is for this reason that when repainting this type of metallic finish, the body shop will do a wide area and fade the paint. Let's say you have a front door replaced. The body shop will likely start at the front fender and repaint most of the entire side of the car so you won't be able to discern where the original paint stopped and the repaint started. The paint is faded in this manner so it's harder to detect. That's why we look at it carefully and walk around it and sight back and forth and move your eyes up and down.

The condition of a used car drastically affects its' value. Due to costs involved, dealers will not fix everything they find wrong with a vehicle. They check for safety concerns such as brakes and seatbelts to be in working and safe condition. These are items that if not done, they can be sued for. Cosmetic items such as paint chips and windshield stars are often passed up or doctored.

If the dealer takes in a car that has rock chips in the paint, he will not usually bother to repaint the surfaces. There is a process of airbrushing that is employed to mask the chips. Let me explain how this works. If you were to magnify the individual rock chip, it would appear as a shallow bowl. In airbrushing, the vendor mixes the paint to match the vehicle color by the paint code on the vehicle. The surface is cleaned and all chips are sprayed with the airbrush. Then a paint remover is applied by hand, using a tightly wrapped, finely woven cloth. Cloth baby diapers used to work about the best! Now this paint remover won't hurt the original finish because it's sealed and thus protected. What does happen is the cloth wipes away all over-spray leaving only the paint held in the chip divot itself. The tightly wrapped cloth glides over the shallow bowl and does not dip inside. It is much like filling a teaspoon with sugar, and running a table knife over the top of the spoon. You will end up with a level teaspoon of sugar.

This process effectively masks the chips, but since this is only a stop gap measure and the paint is not cured as when the surface was actually repainted, it is only temporary. After repeated washings, the paint will work loose and you'll wonder where you got all of those chips in your paint.

Look for signs of this airbrushing when you're inspecting the car. Get down and sight along the hood and fenders. You'll see them. Look carefully and move your eyes around to catch the light. This technique is really inexpensive for a dealer. It will cost anywhere from $20.00 for a hood to around $80.00 for an entire car.

I've seen cars that were literally covered by rock chips; hood, fenders, and top. After airbrushing, you can walk around a vehicle and not even notice these defects at a casual inspection (a nice coat of wax afterward works wonders). Which of course, is the salesperson's strategy — to keep you moving. The airbrushing can also be used to cover scratches on the car. There are also techniques used to fill in gouges on modern plastic or rubber covered bumpers. You must really be careful in your inspection. A complete and professional paint job can cost thousands of dollars and will drastically lower the value of the vehicle, even if done perfectly!

Let's assume that you really like this vehicle and wish to attempt to make a deal. You begin negotiations, but with the understanding that once you agree on how much you will pay, you intend to have the vehicle inspected by your mechanic. Now you can negotiate until you are satisfied with the deal.

The dealer may insist that you do all the paperwork and make it subject to your final approval after the inspection. This is reasonable.

Now, after the inspection, if some repair items come up that are major cost items, you can always re-negotiate with the dealer to either take care of the repairs, or undo the sale. Keep in mind, the dealer may refuse to go any further as it is highly likely the next buyer won't have the car inspected and he can sell it as-is. If he refuses to negotiate further, you know you're at the bottom line, and now you just need to decide whether or not to go ahead. At least you now have the option, and you know any problems you may have to pay out of pocket or live with. The inspection clause allows you to make another offer if you find problems, but once you have negotiated a fair deal, don't be unreasonable in your demands.

Next, take the car to another dealership or an independent shop and pay a mechanic to check it out.

The salesperson will probably have to go with you, but any legitimate dealer will not object to your request. Never deal solely on trust; because the condition of a used vehicle is not a matter of trust, it's a matter of inspecting fully and looking for problems. Maybe the dealer will be surprised by the fact that his own shop missed a bad tranny!

A dealership does not inspect to look for problems when they take a used vehicle in trade. They look to spend the least amount of money possible to make it ready to resell. A used car manager really does not want to hear about a weak engine or transmission that he failed to diagnose. As a used car manager, when I found a bad transmission I didn't want to repair, I would always wholesale the vehicle. However, there are many who will not. Most managers hope that ideally, he can change the oil, give it a bath and unload it on a buyer. Again, the used car manager may have it set up with his shop to just check the obvious items. Many dealers change oil and filter on all used cars, which is more a matter of visual importance to sell the vehicle than actually caring if it's in good condition or not. A great number of customers pull the dipstick on a used car to see how the oil looks. It may not have been changed in 60,000 miles before the dealer just did it. Now Billy Buyer comes along, and looks at it, and is convinced it was well cared for? They also are not going to road test a vehicle, other than maybe to ascertain it doesn't shake you off the road. A slipping transmission will likely pass inspection also, however, as a used car manager; I know that we always were mindful of the spendy problems.

So what about factory certified used vehicles? Certified by whom? A mechanic who is given one hour for a 128 point inspection? Some dealers are more honest about their certified cars than others, but you won't know which ones they are, will you? Factories have stringent inspection and certification processes on paper! No one actually inspects the inspector! That's correct; a factory certified vehicle is actually only inspected by the dealer's regular technicians!

I've seen a lot of the inspections without any service paperwork, where the used car manager sat down at the time of sale and checked off the service checklist for the inspection, signed all the documents and certified the car on paper, but the car never saw the inside of the service department! So much for the validity of certification! Trust only yourself!

A lot of this type of fraud is never known by the car dealer, and a lot of it can never be detected because if there is ever a problem with the vehicle down the road, the certified warranty may pay the repairs and the factory is also never the wiser! This type of cheating is flagrant! So who can you trust? Easy; always inspect what you expect, and trust yourself.

Another thing to keep in mind is the pride and experience of the technician performing the inspection. Maybe on this particular inspection, the technician was having a bad day, or maybe he had already decided to resign his job, and is just going through the motions until he can find another one. How much integrity and care can one expect from a person who hates his job and his employer?

Another thing you need to do is ask the dealer for a CARFAX, which is a history of the vehicle, including previous ownership and whether or not the vehicle has ever had frame damage. If the dealer does not have access to CARFAX, you can access it yourself on the internet. The address is: www.carfax.com. Simply by entering the VIN (vehicle identification number) you can check for a vehicle's salvage history, any odometer fraud, whether it has had multiple owners, any flood damage, major accident damage or fire damage. To see the report will cost you a fee if you do it yourself, but I can't imagine a dealer in this day and age not supplying it to you free. As used car manager, I ran one on every vehicle in stock! From this same screen you can also get a list of CARFAX certified dealers in your area. These dealers use CARFAX reports to guarantee that their used cars have a clean title history. You can run a free lemon check or a free flood damage check. You can also run a free recall check for certain manufacturers.

Be very careful in any purchase of a used vehicle that you research and check it out as carefully as you can. Despite increasing individual state controls and federal laws trying to protect automobile buyers, you can still get taken.

There are people who make their living buying vehicles that have been wrecked and deemed totaled by insurance companies. These vehicles are then purchased and rebuilt by people who have body and mechanical shops just for this purpose. By rebuilding these vehicles and procuring a title for same, they are resold. The individual states are supposed to then issue a title that is clearly stated as *reconstructed*. Then this same vehicle shows up in another state and, this new state issues a title but somehow, miraculously, the new state's title comes out *clean*. No record of any reconstruction. CARFAX was created to protect consumers from this happening. Laundering titles across state lines has been going on continuously even though it's been made more difficult, there are a tremendous number of bad vehicles floating around out there looking for a home. New waves of flood vehicles generally end up in northern states soon after major hurricanes, and with clean titles!

Be especially careful when you're dealing with the small used car lot. Generally speaking, when dealing with a large, well known company connected with a new car franchise, your odds are better that you're going to be protected than with the little guy on the corner lot who has a total investment of 20 cars for sale. He could be gone the next day! That's not to say the big guy can't go away just as quickly, so just be careful before you sign anything! The small guys are generally honest as anyone, but you run a greater risk with them having little or no investment on the line. There are a lot of them that purposely buy these reconstructed vehicles, and they look so nice, and the prices are so low, that many buyers just throw caution to the wind to grab the super deal!

Dealers for the most part are able to function as agents for your state department of motor vehicles and therefore, will take care of transferring legal ownership of your purchase into your name. If you are paying cash for the used car however, there is nothing wrong with you taking possession of the title and taking it to the licensing department yourself. Then you are assured that you will be the legal owner. If you pay cash, and the dealer doesn't do a title transfer and disappears, you may not own a car!

In the very least, you should be allowed to see the title itself. Reason being; oftentimes the car lot may not even have the title! Many dealers operate on the *float*. They have the vehicle on the lot, but do not pay for the car until they sell it. Upon sale, they go to the consignor (generally a wholesaler) and pay for the car to secure the title.

What happens in this case when you pay for the car and this dealer fails to pay the party he received it from? What happens if the wholesaler who consigned it to that dealer has also taken it on consignment from yet another wholesaler or dealer and he doesn't pay for it? You lose! This situation happens regularly around the country.

Next, look at an average new car dealer who takes the used car in on trade and takes the title to his bank and floors it. This means that his bank will accept the title to the used car and add it to the dealer's *floor plan*. In other words, the title becomes collateral for the dealer to borrow operating capital like he does on his new vehicle inventory. Without the availability of this floor plan, most car dealers would not have the money to stay in the used car business. Look at it this way; let's say the dealer sells a new truck that he has *floored* at the bank for $30,000.00. He takes in a trade-in that has a value (ACV) of

$15,000.00. He takes in a difference of $15,000.00 in cash, but to transfer the title to the buyer he needs a total to release it from the bank of $30,000. He has a $15,000.00 trade and only $15,000.00 cash. He is $15,000.00 short! If he has the floor plan available, he can replenish the $15,000.00 by giving the bank the title to the trade-in. Without this available flooring the dealer would have to have enough cash flow to stock the trade-in and wait until it sold before he would have the operating cash back. If a dealer carries an inventory of a million dollars in used vehicles, this is a serious amount of money tied up. This problem carries the same impact percentage-wise for dealers of any size.

Here's an example of what can happen when a dealer goes bad. True story! This dealer carries his floor plan with bank 'A'. He sells a vehicle and finances it through bank 'B'. Bank 'B' pays the dealer his selling price and buys the customer's contract, counting on the dealer to protect them by paying off bank 'A' and filing the title work with the state.

The dealer does not pay off bank 'A'. He does however; take the title to the trade-in to bank 'A' and picks up that cash as well by flooring the trade. Bank 'A' doesn't know this used car came in on trade on their floor-planned new vehicle. This dealer is *running the float*. He has doubled his cash flow, hasn't he? He keeps his profit from the sale, keeps the money by not paying off the vehicle, and he keeps the cash from the used floor-plan amount.

Now multiply this by one hundred. One hundred vehicles sold and the cash only flowed one way, to the dealer! The cash disappears; the dealer goes out of business. Who loses? Well, bank 'A' still has all of the ownership of the vehicles since they've never been paid. They have legal ownership. You finance your car through bank 'B', but bank 'B' doesn't have any title protection. Bank 'A' wants their money or their car. Not your car! Their car! You lose! It's the Golden Rule, "He who has the gold, makes the rules!" The title is the gold!

To protect themselves, banks run floor plan checks periodically. They go to the dealership with a list of all new and used vehicles that they are flooring. The bank wants to make sure that the dealer either has the vehicle in stock and for sale, or if he doesn't, they want their money. If the dealer has sold vehicles and not paid the bank, he is what we call *out of trust*. This is serious as you can see, and can result in the bank taking immediate control of the dealer's assets and his operation.

Dealers who are in financial trouble can get very creative. Another example is a dealer I remember well, who operated a very successful used vehicle sales company in the Midwest. He offered only the nicest used cars, trucks, and R.V.'s. This dealer's reputation was of the highest regard, both with the public and the business community.

The particular bank that carried this dealer's floor plan had a regular schedule of completing their floor plan checks. On the first of every month, like clockwork, the bank employees would show up on the dealer's lot with the lists of cars they were carrying on the floor plan. Generally, the number of vehicles they would have to inspect would range between two hundred and three hundred late model vehicles.

Unbeknownst to the bank, this dealer had slowly gotten himself into financial trouble. He had sold vehicles that he had floored at the bank, but instead of paying them off, he used the money for daily operating expenses and had begun to float. The dealer was able to carry this float over a many month period because he had developed a sophisticated method of covering his tracks.

Since the dealer knew the exact day each month that the bank would arrive for the floor check, he would regularly call the customers that had purchased from him, but where he had not yet paid off the vehicles at the bank, and invite these people in for free oil and maintenance. He arranged for them to drop off their vehicles early in the morning and had his staff shuttle them to their places of employment. Then, license plates were removed, each vehicle was washed, and all personal items removed and put in boxes with the peoples' names on them. The vehicles were put out on the lot as though they were still in stock; prices, stock tags and all. The bankers came right on schedule, completed their inspection, thanked the dealer for his time and went happily back to the bank.

The customers' possessions were then put back in the cars, plates reattached, oil changes, etc. were performed and then the vehicles were given back to the customers when they came in after work. After that, it was business as usual for another month.

During this period, the dealer could see that he wasn't ever going to be able to catch back up, so he started hiding his money. The only vehicles he paid off were ones that financed their purchases through the same bank that had his flooring, or where they arranged for their own financing and he had to produce titles. Also, in the case where license plates were expired and he again had to procure license and title, he necessarily paid them off.

I was working for a large national bank service company at the time, and this bank came under our program. Our job was to supervise their dealer lending and financing programs. Since we were better versed in proper procedures, we restructured this bank's method of operation.

As part of this new procedure, we instructed that floor plan checks needed to be done randomly and never on the same day each month. So, as per the new guidelines, the bank employees were sent back to all of their dealers about three weeks later from their previous floor check. Lo and behold, guess what happened? This dealer's jaw just dropped open. He was caught!

Our employees of course accompanied the banks people on these checks, so when the fact surfaced that this dealer was in an out of trust condition; they immediately took charge of his operation on the spot! Since I was living in the state capitol, I received a call to bring pertinent paperwork such as copies of operation agreements, etc. from the state so the bank could secure all properties and equipment from this dealer. I did so, and brought the U.C.C. (uniform commercial code) filings and helped our people secure the operation before I went home.

The plan was for the dealer to continue doing business and selling his remaining inventory while the bankers and our people would collect all proceeds. We hoped that realizing the retail sales prices on the remaining vehicles that we could cut our losses. That evening at closing, the bank managers closed the dealership, locked the doors and took the keys to all of the vehicles back to the bank and locked them in the vault. Their plan was to return the next day and open the dealership for business and continue liquidating.

Well, after the bankers had a leisurely breakfast the next morning, they drove to — an empty lot! The dealer had been prepared for this possibility and had an extra set of keys for every vehicle. He had moved out over 250 vehicles on convoy trucks overnight! These vehicles disappeared to six different states. He had sold them all! The dealer had some of the titles, and although the bank held the rest, he still had paperwork enough to collect from wholesalers on a promise to furnish titles to these. Most of these recipients were as shady as he was, and they filed phony papers to get new titles.

Our people chased down these vehicles for a full year, and finally gave up on many that never could be found. What a mess. So you can see how something like this could affect your purchase. If the dealer you buy from does not pay for the vehicle you buy from him, you just could wind up losing your trade-in, your newly purchased car, and your money. I've seen a lot of dealers go out of business seemingly overnight, and up until the time they locked the doors, there were no visible indicators.

I'm not trying to dissuade you from buying a used vehicle, just be careful when you do. This can also happen with a new car. As you can see, there is more work to do when you're shopping for a used car. Do your research!

Don't take the dealer's word for the book values either. By that, I mean don't get caught up in the excitement and fail to take a step back before you decide.

Buying a new vehicle is certainly easier because you can research the invoice cost before going out on the market. When looking for a used vehicle, it will require first picking the make and model and then the biggest factor comes in to play; condition!

Now, let's talk some more about negotiating. While you're looking at and driving the used vehicle you're planning to buy, check all of the equipment to make certain it's in working order. Make a note of everything you find wrong. A lot of discussions take place on the lot between the salesperson and the buyer. Promises are implied or made and forgotten just as quickly. Write it down! Of course if you find too many things wrong, you may not even be interested in making any offer. If there are visible defects they didn't bother to fix, what do you suppose waits inside the car? If they don't take care to make sure the obvious faults are handled, how about the internal parts?

If the vehicle has a CD player, ask the salesperson to produce a CD so you can ascertain that it plays. Try the controls to make sure all of the speakers work.

Try the air conditioner. It's hard to tell if the air works in the winter, but lick the tips of your fingers and hold them in front of the air conditioning duct. If you feel a slight stinging, it works, as a general rule. The best way is to make sure the radio is off and the windows are up, so it's quiet, then turn the air on and off and listen for the sound of the air compressor clicking on and off. If you can't hear it, open the hood and have someone else sit in the car and switch the controls. You will see the pulley on the end of the air compressor turn as the switch engages and disengages. Beware of assuming that just because the controls on the dash indicate that there is air conditioning, it may not be in the car!

There have always been manufacturers who have had generic dash board controls. The controls are put there at the factory, but since air conditioning is an option on certain models, the switch may not be connected to anything. It is just the same on the display panel with or without air conditioning.

I know a lot of dealers who got stung on this one by not knowing. Then they sold the vehicle and both dealer and customer thought it had air. The customers upon finding out the truth looked at their contracts and lo and behold, the box for air conditioning was checked on the equipment section of the contract and the dealers had to supply the unit by adding it to the car afterward.

Don't take the chance though. If you can't recognize what an air conditioning compressor looks like, make certain that it's listed on the equipment schedule on the purchase order and any finance documents you sign. I just recently saw a new Ford model that had always had air conditioning as standard equipment that came from a Ford rental return auction that had the dash controls but no compressor. Perhaps it was made for sale in the colder regions. Many years ago, vehicles destined for fleet accounts in the South came in without heaters. Those for the Northern regions came without air conditioners. This kept costs down, but it made it scary on the used vehicle market.

Another caveat you should watch for are the *factory program cars*. You will be told that these are factory lease return vehicles. Leased to whom? The answer is; Hertz, Avis, National, Alamo, and the like. The dealer will want you to think that one individual leased the vehicle and when it came back from this one owner, the manufacturer or lender then sold it to the dealership.

One owner yes, a few thousand drivers probably! How well do you treat a car you rent at the airport? Do you treat it as you would your own? I didn't think so. I don't know very many people who do. People don't treat leased vehicles much better, even if it is a lease to an individual, because they know they aren't keeping it. How much different would they treat the transmission when driving the lease car than they would if they had to end up owning it? Not that people necessarily abuse cars they don't own, but I know driving habits are sure different!

Dealers generally are able to buy these program cars for thousands of dollars below wholesale book value. Does this mean that they're not good cars? Certainly not. It does mean that you should be able to buy them cheaper than you would a regular trade-in. A lot cheaper!

The program cars are generally quite easy to distinguish even if the salesperson doesn't indicate to you that that's what they are. They will usually have most all power options such as power windows, power locks, CD, tilt wheel, cruise control and of course, all have air conditioning. They will be the *middle of the line* cars for that model line. Most will have from 10,000 to the low 20,000's in mileage. A dealer can certainly sell one of these cars for less money than what their true market value is. After all, the car likely has seen more abuse already than you'll ever give it the whole time you own it. Here's where a CARFAX helps you know where the car came from. I will tell you how many owners it had also.

When you negotiate on a program car, you want your first offer to be about $4,000.00 to $5,000.00 below estimated ACV. Even though the potential is there for greater profits, don't ever forget that car people are paid on commission. Sure the next buyer may pay more, but you're there now and the salesperson and manager who are working with you want to be paid something, rather than nothing. The next buyer may work under a different salesperson and manager, so the present staff will want to push their superiors to take any deal now. Customers are not that plentiful and they will fight hard to sell you.

As a manager, and knowing how important it is to keep morale high, I will take the first deal on a vehicle than I can live with. The dealer knows how negative an effect it will create to turn down this salesperson's deal just because he feels he can make more from another customer. You have this reasoning in your favor even though you're making a low offer. A rental return purchase, as I said, may have a great deal more potential profit for a dealer because they will still set the asking price the same as the much nicer cars. When the negotiating is under way, the profit they end up with may not even be as much as any other car, because they want to sell you a vehicle. This is to your advantage to negotiate hard. I always used to tell my people I would take all reasonable offers and consider all unreasonable offers.

Negotiating on a used vehicle is much the same as it is on a new one except it's harder for you to know what the dealer paid for it. You can't research the true cost as you can a dealer invoice.

Researching a used car consists of selecting the makes and models you most like, and you may drive a few of them to help you decide what you like the best. Then it's simply a matter of spending the time to go shopping and take each one as it comes. That is, after you do the following steps.

The research you can do is to determine what the book value is for the make and model you have decided to purchase. The difference being, that when you find one you like, you need to act quickly, because there's only one just like it.

Next, you research consumer guides and the internet, and you come up with the wholesale book value for the year, make, model and average annual miles for said vehicle. Remember, your bank or credit union can supply you with this information as well.

You can look at the classified ads in newspapers and auto sales publications just to see what dealers and private parties are trying to sell them for. Be wary of the private party who is actually a salesperson or wholesaler just selling cars out of his home on the side. He buys vehicles and sells them without transferring the title to his name. Even though state laws generally forbid this practice without a license, if the title isn't transferred, they get away with it. The bad part is that he won't know, or tell you, the vehicle's history and will most likely give you some story that sounds good but it's made up. This particular car might be one the dealer he works for rejected from keeping because there was too much wrong with it. It could have a bad engine, slipping transmission and more. Selling out of his house, you have no one to come back on.

If this seller doesn't have the title in his name, you could be dealing with most anybody. You could be looking at a reconstructed car with a laundered title. Anyway, this section needs to stay devoted to negotiating with the used car dealer. Just be super careful not to blindly trust anyone!

The reason we need to do so much research is because you don't want to pay too much. Our whole objective is to get a better than good deal. There is a need for the dealer to make a profit. This is fine, and we don't begrudge him that. It's just that we don't want it to be excessive! Fair is fair, but who determines fair? That's what you're doing your research for.

What we want to find out is if this particular car you've selected has a good, fair or poor sales rate. If the car you've selected to buy is one of those that dealers can buy for $5,000.00 less than the wholesale (low book) value, then we certainly don't want to offer to purchase this vehicle for even close to low book.

Check the ads carefully. Call some of the private party ads. If you find they all still own them, then they are obviously priced too high or they would have sold. Dealer prices in the newspaper must be low enough to attract buyers or they could save their money by not advertising them at all. When running used car ads, if a dealer owns several of the same year, make, and model, he will naturally advertise the worst one of the group. That's the one with the highest miles, least equipment, and worst condition. Because of this, don't assume that these are necessarily the prices that you can expect on every other similar car. You are just making comparisons at this time.

Another fact to be aware of is, the timing of your purchase can affect the price you ultimately end up paying. Dealers must periodically *turn* their inventory. By this, I mean the length of time a used vehicle remains in stock. Ideally, for the most profitable used car operation, a vehicle that remains on the lot over 45 days is a potential liability. Because of the fact that used car guide books change every month or two, the actual wholesale value goes down, and therefore, so does the amount that a lender will finance on this vehicle. Also, we have seasonal vehicles. Yes, this has a direct bearing.

Just a side note; boat dealers make a much better profit in the winter because the consumers believe they get better deals in the off-season. Just the opposite of what logic would dictate; winter is God's gift to boat dealers!

In the automobile business, since we must turn our inventories, we can't take in a convertible in the winter and keep it until late spring when the market gets strong. Most car dealers make their used car managers limit the time they can keep a vehicle in stock to 60 to 90 days or less. Therefore, if we take a convertible in trade in the fall or winter months, we are going to own it for a lot less than we would stock it in for in the spring. Conversely, the four wheel drive sport utility vehicle becomes worth a lot more in October than it is in May, so you can see that seasons can make you, or cost you money, depending if you're buying or selling.

I've purchased millions of dollars in vehicles from dealer auto auctions and from wholesalers and I will always pay more for a convertible in the spring and not be interested, even at a steal, in the winter. Of course my career has been in our Northeast, Midwest and Northwest, so you can see my slant will be different than the California dealer who has a much stronger convertible market all year 'round, and the Texas dealer who wouldn't want a 4X4 if you gave it to him! You just have to adapt strategies to the market you live in, as a dealer must.

Consumers are also affected by transfers from one part of the country to another. Say you're living in Dallas, Texas and you purchase a two wheel drive Ford Explorer. It works fine until you get that transfer to Denver, Colorado, where a two wheel drive sport utility is almost sale proof, because in essence it's just a passenger van! Seasons and geographic locations dramatically affect vehicle values.

Once you have a general idea of prices asked and the wholesale (low) book value of the vehicle you want to buy, negotiations will be the same as with the new car.

Dealing is dealing, so proceed with your plan and don't be afraid to walk out a few times if necessary, and if you do, do it courteously.

A lot of sales happen after the customer drives away. Good salespeople follow up with potential buyers. Even if their manager just walks away from you, the salesperson is affected more directly and with greater financial impact by selling you a car! They will follow up after you leave, so be prepared to negotiate a little more when they phone you. Just flex a bit, and the salesperson will take it to the manager and try to make a deal.

I've seen salespeople and closers go to different sales managers and try to work around the original appraisers in order to put a deal together. Reason being is, as we looked at before, every manager who appraises a trade-in will have a different opinion on its value. For this reason, if your salesperson doesn't follow up with you, it may be very smart of you to follow up with them; especially if you were close to making a deal when you left. Your salesperson may have felt you were lost forever, and now you call, and they will get very creative in a hurry! Trust me; it's a very smart thing to do! If the salesperson doesn't call you back, he may not be smart enough to follow up on his customers. Don't let his ignorance stop you from making a deal. Also, inexperienced salespeople are more timid, and don't want to insult you by being pushy, and some are just lazy. Remember, you're in charge of what happens, so you make the call!

CHAPTER 9
LEASING — THE TRUTH AND THE LIES

"The **leased** important people make the dealer the **most** profits!"

Let us now look at the most misunderstood and often the most abused facet of the automobile business; leasing.

To begin with, let's un-complicate leasing by reducing it to what it actually is in its' simplest terms: A lease is a *contractual rental of property*, for a specified time at a given dollar amount.

When you lease, *you do not* enter into an agreement to purchase. You enter instead, into a contract to use a vehicle for a given period of time and then give it back. At the end of the lease period, you may have an *option* to purchase the vehicle, as when you finish this chapter, you will see that they want you to exercise this option!

As in a finance contract, the dealer does the paperwork with you and then sells (assigns) the lease to a bank or special lease company who is called the *lessor*. You are called the *lessee*. The difference between the lease and the purchase is that when you sign a regular finance contract, you are the buyer and when you have completed your obligation, the vehicle's title will belong to you. When you lease, the lessor is actually the purchaser of the vehicle and the lessor will be shown on your registration as the legal owner of the vehicle.

Now let's further un-complicate leasing by understanding how it is done. When you lease, there are several factors that go into the calculations. First of all, a determination must be made as to how much of the vehicle's value will be *used up* during the lease term. That amount is called the *depreciation*. Depreciation is calculated by multiplying the manufacturers' suggested retail price (MSRP) by a depreciation-percentage. This percentage is arrived at by the history of that particular make and model as to how much of its' original value (MSRP) it retains after a given amount of time. The reason that MSRP is used as the base is that this figure is a constant and does not vary like dealer pricing does.

For example, let's take a particular vehicle that is three model years old and has 36,000 miles, average condition and is selling through automobile auctions at an average price of $20,000.00. Records show that three years ago when this vehicle was brand new, the MSRP was $40,000.00. History of this vehicle therefore indicates that it will lose half of its' original *sticker* price in three years. Unless other factors would indicate that this model is losing favor with purchasers, it would be reasonable to assume that a depreciation percentage would still be fifty percent on current models. If it loses fifty percent of its' value, that means that at the end of a three year lease, the remaining value should also be fifty percent of original MSRP. This remaining or end value is called the *residual*.

In calculating a lease, therefore, the first thing done is to estimate this residual value. If a particular vehicle has an end (or residual) value of 45% then it will lose 55% of its' original list (MSRP) price. This depreciation amount is the basis for your monthly payment.

We all know that a vehicle does not depreciate at an even rate. In actuality it depreciates the most the first year, less the second year and so on. If you have a vehicle that will lose fifty-five percent of its' value in three years, chances are it will lose thirty-five percent the first year and the other twenty percent over the next two years. That's reality!

Now in calculating a lease, the lessor cannot base your lease payments on actual depreciation or your payment schedule would start out extremely high and would be much lower later on in the contract.

Understanding the percentage of original MSRP that will be lost over a given period of time (depreciation) gives us the percentage of value that will be remaining (residual.) This residual value is the percentage that will first be used in a lease calculation. If you have a vehicle that will lose an estimated 55% of its value over three years, then it will have a residual (remaining) value of 45%.

This 45% is multiplied times the current MSRP of the vehicle you are leasing. Keep in mind, calculating the residual has no bearing on what you will offer for a price you will lease for. It must be calculated this way because not everyone pays MSRP! Some pay more, most pay less. The selling price of a leased vehicle *must still be negotiated*. If you don't negotiate, you're paying too much! A great many customers think there's something magical about a lease and they just think the numbers are what they are and don't even realize they have the ability to negotiate them! For this reason, dealer's love leasing! Customers have always been easier to close on a lease because they got what they wanted — no negotiating!

Anyway, in calculating the lease, you take whatever *selling price you* arrive at and subtract the residual value. The difference is the *depreciation*. Divide the depreciation by the term of the lease (months) and you have your *base lease payment*.

When you look carefully at a lease, you see that the lessor now will calculate interest on this base payment the same as they would on any installment loan. Since you will be making regular payments on this amount, they will be receiving their money on a declining balance. Each month, the amount owing is reduced by your base monthly payment amount.

But what about that residual balance? I'm glad you asked. When the lease is purchased by a lessor, the lessor pays the dealer the full sale price for the vehicle. Now, they lease it to you. A bank or lease company always makes a profit on any amount they loan, so now in case you forgot about that residual or end value; they didn't. You are going to pay a *fixed rate* of interest on that residual balance for the whole term of the lease. Let's say for example that your lease is for three years and the residual is $20,000.00. It would be the same as if you borrowed $20,000.00 from your bank with the agreement that you would keep the money for three years and then repay the loan with three years of interest in one lump sum at the end.

A lot of commercial and farm loans are done on an annual basis, and that's just how the lease residual works. Your interest costs are a lot greater this way because the balance is staying at the same amount, although it makes the payment lower. Unlike a regular loan where you make a monthly payment and are therefore paying interest on a lesser amount each month. On a declining balance, you will have paid back roughly half of the loan when you are half way through the contract and for this reason, you pay about half the interest you would on a fixed balance.

The lease residual is a fixed balance for the entire term of the lease. Interest is calculated on your having that amount of money for the term of the lease and rather than collect the charges at the end, they are added into your monthly payment.

So you see, to calculate a lease payment, the steps are to calculate the depreciation amount and the interest on this amount on a monthly payment basis and interest added for the residual loan.

Next, we must add to the lease other charges. A lease *acquisition fee* is charged by the lessor and is an extra profit for them, like a loan fee. It always makes me wonder why the lenders don't always charge a loan fee if the dealer prepares a finance contract but they sneak in an acquisition fee on a lease. Probably, because people are easier to sell the fee to on a lease because they feel it's something special. In reality, it is just an extra gouge.

The most common lease you will run across today is the *closed-end* or *walk away* lease. This means that the residual value is fixed and that you as the lessee are not responsible for that value at the end of the lease. You are only responsible for abnormal wear and tear, and excess miles.

A few years back, there were still open-end leases available around the country. With an open-end lease a payment can be tailored to the needs of the lessee by changing the residual. You can see that if the residual value is increased, the amount of depreciation is less and therefore the payment is lower. The catch though, is that at the end of the lease the lessee is responsible for the residual. If the end-value is less than estimated, the lessee must pay the difference. You don't want an open-end lease, believe me! It's like being able to select a payment you like, and making up for it at the end!

The typical closed-end lease that we are dealing with today offers the lessee a purchase option at the lease-end. Be careful to read the documents up front, because there is more often than not a glossed over and most often undisclosed charge at lease end if you decide you wish to purchase the vehicle at the residual value. This could cost an extra several hundred dollars, just to exercise your purchase option.

This lease end *purchase fee* is another rip off adding more profit to the banks' end. The lessor doesn't want your vehicle back at lease end, because they're not in the car business, and to them this is a liability. Ideally for the lessor is to have you trade it in before the lease is up. So why do they charge you for helping them dispose of a potential problem? Because lease customers are the easiest to snow, because they don't read the fine print! They are, for the most part, more trusting of a lease than they would be in a financed purchase, because they believe leasing is somehow controlled for their protection. Not!

Lease interest and profit are calculated as you see, but the terms are disclosed as either an interest rate or a "money factor." You will seldom see any of the lease calculations, but you need to ask *what interest rate is being used* to calculate your lease. If they lie by telling you, "We don't use an interest rate, but a money factor," they are trying to con you—leave! You may give them a chance to be straight, as this line they give you is a rehearsed *lease pitch*.

Knowing that your credit rating qualifies you for a loan rate of five percent (5%) you wouldn't think it right that you should pay 8% for a lease, would you? So what do you do if the dealer tells you that the lease is calculated with a rate of 5.4? Sounds good right? Ask them if this is a true interest rate or a *money factor*? This is where you can get taken! A huge percentage of dealer employees don't really even know the difference! They quote the factor as a rate, which is grossly incorrect!

The average manager in a car dealership doesn't even have the basic understanding of a lease that I just explained to you. They look at the lessor supplied residual value guide, enter that percentage in the computer, then they enter the money factor, MSRP, selling price, cash down, etc., and the lease is calculated. These managers and dealers would have no conception of how to hand calculate your lease. Even those who have a remote idea of how a lease works are not going to fully disclose items such as the acquisition fee, or the charge to purchase the vehicle at lease-end. Seldom have I found any manager in a dealership who has ever read a lease contract. Everything today is so programmed into the computer that the dealer doesn't even have residual charts anymore. He just pushes buttons.

Then, you can run into the deception that is purposely done! Now, you are working against both ignorance and cunning, so you have to face a dual problem. Even if the person you're dealing with is entirely honest, you could still face a problem due to the fact that he or she might not be the one who's actually doing the calculations, such as operations who employ the use of a closer or if the person working directly with you is not the one who's working the computer. They may not be receiving the full disclosure. Besides, during the negotiations, a lot of things may be brushed over, not disclosed, or otherwise exaggerated, so just make sure you review everything before you sign the completed documents!

Let us now go back to the point where the dealer tells you the rate on your lease is 5.4% or says you are getting a 5.4% lease rate. Ask to be certain, "Is this a money factor?" If they tell you it's a money factor, then multiply that percentage by 2400. 5.4% equates to a decimal equivalent of .0054, so enter .0054 into your calculator, and multiply it times 2400, and your answer is 12.96%. This is the actual interest your lease is being calculated at! That's nuts! Keep this calculation handy if you're thinking of leasing. Where does all that interest go?

Realize now, that the dealer is allowed by the lessor to add profit into the interest rate, as he can on a standard finance contract. The bank or lease company will pay the difference in the rate charged, to the dealer. This is a huge profit center for a dealer. Unbeknownst to the consumer, the dealer still makes enormous finance profits on leasing!

So let's work this multiplier in reverse. On your calculator, do a reverse procedure as follows: Take a rate you know you can qualify for on a loan, say 5%. Divide 5.0 by 2400 and you have .00208. Tell the dealer that you expect a money factor of .00208 and don't accept anything higher! This will let you calculate the payment and save you a "ton of money!" If you qualify for an interest rate of 6%, divide 6 by 2400 and your money factor should be .0025.

It's best to wait on this until you are in with the finance manager because he will have in front of him the actual *lease worksheet* that will accompany the lease to the lessor. Insist on seeing it and have him walk you through the actual calculations, as you will not be shown this worksheet by whoever is closing your transaction.

There will be a lease acquisition fee that the bank will assess as part of your charges. Look on this as a loan fee, and ask if it can be removed? Otherwise, it will be part of your monthly payment. You're stuck with that, but Lessors will also allow dealers to add around $300.00 or so to this lease fee, and of course the extra going back to the dealer, so always resist on the acquisition fee and you can negotiate it also. This is pure back-end profit, plus; any amount the dealer can get you to pay by raising the interest rate or money factor! The extra profit on the back-end that the dealer makes on a lease cannot be lost as it can on a finance contract if the customer pays it off early. With a finance contract, the dealer receives a charge-back on his finance reserve account, if you prepay the contract. But with the lease he keeps the excess that he charged you and you pay a pre-payment penalty on top of it, for early lease termination! A lease is not designed for trading out early. If you do, you will pay blood!

If you pay off a lease early, bend over and grab your ankles! You will suffer huge prepayment penalties. When you enter into a lease, you'd better make sure you plan to drive the vehicle through the full term of the lease agreement, and don't even consider otherwise, no matter what future plans you may have.

Do I recommend leasing? No! Emphatically no! In case you couldn't see how I really feel, I'll quit beating around the bush; I do not believe that leasing will do any more than hurt the average consumer!

Let's explore further. Of course car dealers will try to push you into a lease because their potential profit is so much greater! The average consumer does not understand leasing and they have a fear of it because of the horror stories they've heard. Give me enough time to make my presentation and I'll convince the majority of customers that the lease is the best way to go. I'll make it look so attractive, dispel all of your fears, and show you such a beautiful picture that you'll wonder where leasing has been all your life!

When giving the pitch on a lease, we will have already checked your credit to make sure you can qualify. The average lessee must generally have a somewhat higher credit score in order to qualify, but no different than those who can finance at a good rate. The reason for this higher credit requirement is that banks will usually lend a higher dollar amount on a lease than their guidelines call for on a finance contract, and so the credit worthiness of a lessee needs to be better! As an example, say on a finance contract, the lender may finance 100% to 115% of the invoice cost, but on a lease they may very well finance 125% or more of the MSRP. It is for this reason that car dealers like leases so much, because we can make more money, without bigger down payments! Also, if you can't come up with enough down payment money for a dealer to make maximum profit on a purchase, he may *switch you* to a lease, where he can increase the profit yield.

Oftentimes, we have a tough time making regular financing work because the customer has so much *negative equity* in the trade-in. Without a large amount of cash down, we may be limited to how much profit we can make, only because of how much the lender will finance. We need to make the maximum profit, so a switch to a lease is the best approach for the dealer in this case. We always try to close you on the lease idea because it is so easy to get all the profit!

A lot of people don't care so much about the monthly payment if they can make an easy transaction. These people are prime candidates to switch to a lease because I can finance a higher balance and increase my profit. Another reason a lease is so easy to sell is because the majority of customers, as I've said before, are payment buyers.

If I come out with two columns of numbers, plan A and plan B and plan B looks so much better, it'll certainly open up the conversation, won't it? Look at this example of an actual presentation to a customer:

Plan A	Plan B
Dealer to pay off $5,500.00 trade (your balance)	Dealer to pay off $5,500.00 trade (your balance)
$3,500.00 cash down	$1,000.00 cash down
72 months X $574.00	60 months X $425.00

Now, based on your first look at these figures, doesn't plan B just seem too good to be true?

You'll notice of course that no trade allowance is addressed, just the amount that must be paid off to *secure title* to the customer's vehicle, the down payment, and the monthly payments. Certainly, plan B looks so much better. Both plans, of course, have a higher payment than is needed, as a test the water trial, but the purchase plan A is even more packed, (the payment is raised out of proportion to reality) to make it more unattractive at the onset than the Plan B (lease).

With the customer's interest being sparked by the lower down payment, lower monthly payments, and shorter term, the lease presentation can begin. Most customers will at this point, try to turn a deaf ear to any further talk of leasing. The first objection we hear will likely be, "I want to own my car." To which in this case, we reply, "You don't own the one you're trading in, the bank does." If further discussion of a lease seems out at this point, we resume negotiations on the purchase, as though we have accepted the customer's decision. We will push hard for down payment, monthly payment and return to the sales office with the customer's counter-offer, only to purchase, not lease.

In most instances, unless the customer is absolutely adamant about not leasing and gets to the point of open hostility at being pushed, the (dealer proposals) pencils will still come back each time showing both plans, A and B.

We will keep on showing each successive offer to highlight the lease advantage, and gently keep touting the virtues of a lease. If you do desire to lease, and you purchased or financed your current vehicle, you may have a tax credit coming.

Since sales tax is calculated normally on the actual lease payment, you are not paying tax on the entire purchase amount like you do when you finance or pay cash. For this reason, if you live in a sales tax state, you paid tax on that full price, or the difference of the price after trade, when you got you present car, and now should receive a tax credit for the current trade in value of this vehicle. The dealer calculates how much tax credit is due you, and since the new sales tax is based on the payment amount, that's how you will get the tax credit returned to you.

Say the monthly tax on your lease payment is $45.00 and your total payment comes to $550.00 including this tax. If you have a $1,000.00 tax credit, divide the $1,000.00 by the $45.00 and this means you won't have to start making the monthly tax payments for 22 months. Now for almost two years, your payment will only be $505.00. Make sure this is done properly before you sign anything. A lot (an awful lot) of dealer managers do not understand this tax credit and don't give the lessee the proper credit. If they don't calculate it accurately, you will lose it! The state keeps it. Automobile sales managers are normally not up to par on doing leases, and when you go from purchase to a lease, they are most likely to either not know how, or not care. After all, it's only your money!

This is especially dangerous for customers living in a sales tax state, and buying across state lines from a non-sales tax state.

Anytime I could start off with much lower payments, without them going up for two or three years, what an advantage! Most payment buyers always feel things will be easier down the road, so lower payments now are an easy sell, if it's later on before they increase.

The vast majority of customers who lease have no idea as to how to keep the dealer honest when leasing a vehicle. In most states today, the capitalized cost (sales price) of the lease is disclosed and appears on the lease document.

Just a few years ago it did not! Can you imagine how easy it was to cater to the person who wanted a specific trade allowance, say $10,000.00 for a vehicle worth only $5,000.00. This was perfect for the dealers' disclosure, as all they had to show on the lease was the trade allowance. There was no selling price (capitalized cost), ever shown on the lease document.

Many times, I saw this exact example happen. A customer came in to look at a new luxury vehicle, and he had been all over town, and his only real problem what that no one was giving him what he wanted for his trade-in. The dealer started out by convincing him that he would be best served by leasing, and that he never again would have to worry about trade values.

He agreed, but stated that he would do the transaction only with the proper trade-in on his present vehicle. Everyone else had been $5,000.00 short of what he wanted. Simple, this dealer raised the selling price on the lease worksheet by $5,000.00, and gave him what he wanted for his trade allowance. Since the only number he saw in writing was the trade, he was ecstatic, and they made a full ++ profit! Everybody was happy! I saw this happen daily! It took far too long for states to require full disclosure. Prior to that it was a *license to steal*! That's the reason leasing was so hated by consumers who found out how they got hurt after it was too late. Even now, the lease document is too hard for the consumer to decipher.

Take the good negotiator who ends up with a capitalized cost of $100.00 over invoice. How can this lessee know how much the dealer is really making in back-end profit? The lessee is happy because he only paid a $100.00 profit to the dealer, and then paid him a $2,000.00 profit he wasn't aware of! Everyone is happy! "Y'all come back now, hear!"

Some manufacturers have their own finance institutions. These include Toyota Finance, Nissan Motor Acceptance, Ford Motor Credit, BMW, Volkswagen, Chrysler Credit, and others.

Sometimes these captive companies will give unusually high residual values in order to promote higher sales of their vehicles. By raising the residuals on their leases, the amount of estimated depreciation goes down, resulting in a lower monthly payment, which increases sales! They of course know that at the end of the lease period that the returning vehicle won't be worth the residual, but when they get it back, they can write off the loss after they ultimately sell it. There goes any sensible way the buyer has of completing the purchase, because it won't be worth anywhere close to the residual, and a person would be a fool to buy it at lease end! The lease company, of course, will be working hard to get the lessee to complete the purchase prior to lease-end. You likely will be barraged with offers to finance the residual balance at a low interest rate if you buy out your lease. The lease company is able to offer the great finance rates, as the odds show that even if a person buys out his lease, he soon trades it off anyway, so even if you take advantage of a low interest rate as an incentive, you'll likely trade soon, and they're saved!

Import manufacturers have long been accused of *dumping* vehicles into our U.S. market by these methods! They also hope that you may trade it off before the lease is up, thus getting them off the hook.

Certainly, trading out of a lease before it is completed will have prepayment penalties, but in the case of the true payment buyer, he does not really care about all of the details, negative equity, penalties, or anything else. As long as he can live with the cash down needed, and handle the monthly payment, he's in. This, after all, is our bread and butter buyer, and we know how to cater to his whims. The automobile industry owes its' success almost entirely to the ease in which people can buy and lease cars!

Have you leased before and wanted a 36 month lease, but by the salesperson showing you the lower payment, you accepted an odd-term such as 39 months? Do you think the lessor did that for your benefit? Wrong! They plan for you to *trade out* of it in three years so they won't have to get it back and take a chance on selling it. How?

Their thinking is that at the end of 36 months, you will realize that you must pay to re-license the vehicle for another year or more, and faced with that expense with only three months to go on your lease anyway, that you'll just go ahead and trade it in early rather than wait. Slick, huh? There aren't any real apparent penalties because you're trading it in with only three months to go, so your three payments plus the residual value is your payoff. Where your penalty comes in is that you are essentially forced into; completing your purchase of the leased vehicle at too huge a residual price! In order for you to trade-out of the vehicle, you must own it, therefore, the new dealer pays off your lease that has a ridiculously high residual and you absorb this difference (negative equity) in your new transaction! This will cost you a bunch! You never would have considered buying your leased vehicle, and now because of an innocent appearing three extra months, you just got taken! Now you are carrying a higher payment on your new car due to a high residual payoff!

Another example is a certain luxury sports car that advertises 27 month leases. This works the same way, the payment difference between a 24 month lease and a 27 month lease may be slightly lower, but here again, the lessor knows that when your vehicle license plates are due that you will still have three months to go on your lease. They hope that you will lease a new one, complete the purchase, or trade it to someone else, anything so the lessor won't get it back! I have had lease companies and banks acknowledge to me that this is why they use 27, 39, 42, 51, 63, and all sorts of odd terms. The best gift you could give the lessor is to complete the purchase!

A lessor relies upon past experience in setting lease terms and expirations. Experience with car buyers has shown that the new car smell wears of within six months after taking delivery! With most people, the excitement of a new car soon fades, and as soon as the payments begin, and it gets its' first scratch, the love affair fades fast.

Now a lessee that is faced with re-licensing a vehicle with only a few months 'til lease-end, will not be likely to spend much thought as to the consequences and will most often just go car shopping again. Instead of being able to walk away from the lease, this unfortunate individual defeats the entire purpose of the lease, and goes in somewhere to trade out.

As I mentioned in the beginning, if you are going to lease; lease short term, and be prepared to walk away when it's over. A lessee in this scenario would be better off to just pay the last three payments and turn the vehicle back early, but thanks to America's love affair with cars, people get caught up in the shopping and take the easy way out. Many people also fear being without a car, or being inconvenienced even a tiny bit by having to drop off the leased rig and getting something new. This is what the lessor counts on. You trade it and take your beating!

So rather than receive any benefit from a lease, whose residual is unrealistically high, and creating a lower payment than should have been; our hapless buyer now pays it all back! All of the payment savings from the too high residual is now sacrificed when he trades it in instead of turning it back! All over three months of license renewal fees! That's how lessors dump vehicles in our market and get away with it.

As we know, a lessee must first own it in order for him to trade it, and therefore, the dealer calls the lessor for a payoff. The payoff may even include extra profit penalties for prepayment and so forth, but our typical payment buyer just turns the other cheek, and comes away with a disdain toward leasing, and accepts a long term finance contract and drives away in his new car. Now he's going to pay more interest on the negative equity and over a longer period of time, because the new dealer blames it all on that bad, bad lease, and buries him all over again.

Be wary, and think of this when you are approached with leasing as an option. If it's so honest and above board, then why do they find it necessary to set the lessee up for a future problem? Do not lease for any odd term. Coincide any lease with the license plate renewal! This all comes back to; NEVER BUYING A LEASE VEHICLE at the lease end!

If you should be in a position where you have three months to go on a lease, and your license plates are due for renewal, you're probably better off to write a check for the three payments and turn it back in to the lessor. Of course you could buy the new registration and pay the next three payments and continue driving the vehicle until termination, but it's a lot better not to let them shaft you with this in the first place. Lease only for an even annual term!

Despite the fact that I think it's a poor choice; the other option is to complete the purchase. The safe way to go about this, is, prior to lease-end, you go about "shopping" the leased vehicle. Just like if you owned it and want to trade it in, you need to establish an actual cash value (ACV). If you find that used car dealers will pay you close to what your purchase option on this leased vehicle would be, then you would be buying it (wholesale), and since you are the one who has been driving it the whole time, it may be a smart purchase. Most lessees will not be interested in purchasing their leased vehicle however, because they most likely lease so they can continue driving new cars every time, without the hassle of trade-ins.

If you lease a vehicle that has a reputation for being long lasting, you may be wise to complete the purchase, if you have decided for sure that you will drive this vehicle for years more.

It's not too likely that the purchase option (residual) on a luxury car will be close to the ACV (actual cash value) anyway, so you probably don't have to worry about one of those being a bargain. You know how I feel about leases, but the ease of the lease transaction (a lot of leasing is done through the fleet department), makes people prefer the process over all the negotiating through the sales process. Just make certain you are treated fairly. Oftentimes, a lease company is open to offers for less than the residual; they really don't want it back! You may call the lessor, and ask if they will give you a lower purchase price than the stated residual.

Include in this mix, the person who receives a car allowance from his or her company. They lease, as long as it fits their budget (payment buyers). Unless you are a very shrewd negotiator, you will pay more to lease than it will cost you to purchase. You will be forced to carry higher automobile insurance limits than average, because the lease company wants higher coverage to protect their interests, as well as your own.

If you are one who just wants a new vehicle every two years and cannot handle the negotiations, then at least negotiate a better deal on the lease (see the worksheet) and review and question the capitalized cost). This figure is what you are actually paying for the vehicle.

The dealer will tell you, "You're not actually buying the car," and he's correct. What you are doing though is negotiating what the vehicle is being sold to the lease company for. So since the lease company only purchases the vehicle from the dealer after you negotiate the deal, then you are paying for it. You alone are responsible for what the lease company pays for the vehicle, and you alone, are negotiating your costs of the lease! All the lease company does is write the dealer a check when you're done making your deal! Maybe your employer is leasing the car for you, and you aren't concerned about the payment. Just remember, the harder you negotiate, the more car you can get for the same payment.

Another thing you need to think about if you do decide to lease. Never put a down payment up front! A lot of leases are advertised with X dollars up front and the resulting lower payment. Other than first payment, (always up front) and license and title fees, there is no good reason for down payment on a lease!

If you are doing so to reduce your monthly payment, then you shouldn't be leasing in the first place! Do not ever use a trade-in to reduce your monthly payments on a lease! Take cash back instead if you have a trade-in. That's right, if you have a paid for trade, settle on what you will accept for the car, and take a check back instead! Do not use it for down payment! Ever! And, to again repeat myself, never ever pay money down on a lease!

Okay, so why not use cash or trade allowance up front to lower your payments on a lease? Say you put all this money into the lease, and then you have an accident, and the vehicle is totaled. You will have the vehicle replaced by the insurance, but the lease is done! Unless the lease company will allow a substitution vehicle, which they may not, you must now negotiate a new lease, and the residuals and money factors (interest rates) may have drastically changed against you! Suddenly, leasing may no longer be to your advantage, but you already lost your cash and trade for a lower payment, which now does you no good because it is all gone! So if you have, let's say for example, put $3,000.00 cash down on the lease to get a lower payment, and the lease company can't or won't allow a vehicle replacement by your insurance company, you just lost your money that you put down for lower payments, which are now cancelled.

If you feel you must reduce your monthly lease payment in order to afford it, then my advice would be to still keep your cash! That's right, keep your money in the bank, and take cash for your trade-in. Put it all in the bank, and dip into your reserve when you need it to put toward your payment. A lower payment also does you no good if you trade early, but the cash on hand would definitely be an advantage!

If you were in a purchase agreement rather than a lease, and if the lender should not allow a substitution vehicle, the situation shouldn't cost you. Your advantage is that using a down payment or trade-in on a purchase gives you a lower balance financed, and it's easy to start anew.

Not only am I totally against down payments on a lease; I am also totally opposed to long term leases. If you must lease, then lease for only as long as you intend to use the vehicle. Never, ever lease for a longer term with the intention of trading vehicles before the lease term ends. You are just kidding yourself if you do this.

I'll quit beating on leases with a final comment: If you must satisfy your ego by driving more vehicle than you really should be, then finance it for a longer term if necessary, but do not lease it.

If you need money down on a lease, then face the reality; you can't afford it. Don't take chances on something that can have such an impact on your future credit standings. Remember, if it takes cash down to make a deal work, take it as a warning; you're getting in too deep.

Always keep in mind; to pay off a lease early, you pay all of the finance profit for the entire remaining term! To pay off a purchase, you pay interest only on the unpaid balance until the day you pay it off. No prepayment penalty!

Looking back, at just one example; There was a time that sport utility vehicles, such as Chevrolet's Tahoe and Suburban were almost *bullet proof* (financially). They were almost always worth more than their residuals. The banks in realizing this, and in order to be more competitive, kept the residual values high in order to attract lease business. Remember, high residual = lower payment. When General Motors began filling the pipelines and every dealer had an abundance of these sport utes, the market values plummeted and the banks were stuck with all of these vehicles coming off lease with values not anywhere near the residuals that they owned them for, and knowing this, the lessees were not considering purchasing at the lease end, they were all walking away. The same thing happened when Ford Motor Company created the Excursion. This huge urban assault looking vehicle looked like the perfect answer to the ultimate SUV. It came out and immediately fizzled!

Who can judge the future market? That's one thing about a lease that could be a benefit in disguise. When you lease, you don't have to speculate on the future value of the vehicle. The lessor does. If at the lease end, the vehicle is worth more on a wholesale basis than your purchase option (residual), then buy it and turn around and sell it. Pocket the difference. If it's worth less than its' residual, you just walk away! Another pitfall of leasing is the mileage limitation penalty that leases come with. You can have a lessor increase your mileage allowance but your payment will go up. It stands to reason that if a residual value is calculated based on the returning vehicle having 36,000 miles on it, then if that same vehicle actually comes back with 48,000 miles, it will be worth less money. Residual values are affected directly by estimated condition and mileage calculated up front, and the actual condition and mileage at lease end determine the true ACV.

Most customers that are sold on the lease did not come in with the idea to lease. Since they have been converted to leasing, the mileage penalties are something the dealer discloses, but they do not elaborate on it. When the lessee voices concern about driving more miles than the standard 12 to 15,000 per year, the dealer will make light of it with statements like, "You only pay a penalty if you turn it back to the bank, which of course, you never want to do." "You'll either trade it, sell it or buy it!" or, "Based on our past experience with this model, it will hold its' value so well that even with more miles you can't get hurt." Remember this paragraph! It is a standard lease pitch lie!

What a crock! Get to the end of this lease and have 48,000 miles, which is 12,000 miles over the schedule, have a 15 cents per mile penalty, which equals $1,800.00 and now you also have to pass a vehicle inspection by the lessor, just in order to pay through the nose and be able to walk away! Remember, the penalty is chiseled in stone. Now the lessor can also take you to task for 12,000 more miles of wear and tear. That's correct! In addition to a mileage penalty, you must let them inspect it! What happens to so many people when they start building up the mileage is they switch to driving another vehicle if they can, and just let the leased vehicle sit. What a waste! All because of trying to save money on a payment, by allowing the dealer to con them into a lower estimated mileage allowance.

Are the tires in need on replacing? They may not be without the extra miles, but you are always responsible, and the tires must be good when you turn it back in! Does it have any scratches, tears in the upholstery, stains on the carpet, cracked glass? You can count on being charged for any excessive wear and tear in addition to the mileage penalty. Yes, this includes repainting for rock chips, etc. Anything that the lessor can argue that is not normal wear!

This example of a typical sales pitch on leasing is all designed to further convince you of how nice it will be to lease. Take the line, "You only pay a mileage penalty if you turn it back to the bank, which of course, you never want to do." First of all, with excess mileage, they charge you a penalty because the vehicle having excess miles is worth less than it should be. Even if you could sell it yourself, and not turn it back to the bank, you'd get less for it because of this factor, so you pay for it regardless!

You won't sell it, you won't complete the purchase, you won't trade it, because you will get hurt with all of these options! Anytime your dealers' people start using these sales pitches; they are lying to you! They are trying to con you into a stupid decision. No matter how much you are trying to cut corners in your projected driving habits to afford the payment, don't! You will always lose!

Now for another huge reason to avoid leases! I can't count how many cases I've seen where peoples' lifestyle changes abruptly, and without warning! What happens if you lose your job and find another that is 30 more miles away? That's 60 more miles a day, and 15,600 per year, in addition to what you were already driving. This happens all the time. What happens if a spouse loses a job due to illness? Any type of change in the family income can be more devastating when you're leasing because of early termination penalties. If you think the lessor will have a sympathetic ear, forget it!

So now you think back to what the dealer told you, "You'll trade it, buy it, or sell it." Of course that statement turns out to be true because you won't be able to afford to pay all the penalties to return it to the lease company at the lease end.

You now are forced to trade in a vehicle with above average miles, which of course is worth less than the residual value which is now your payoff. Also, now you are forced to assume responsibility for the residual value of this vehicle which was what you hoped to avoid by leasing it in the first place, and to be able to walk away at the end of the lease.

Also, what if the vehicle wouldn't have been worth its' residual value even if the miles had been under the limit? Then you could have been free of it. Now, you're just going to pay even more of a penalty if it is necessary to dispose of the vehicle prior to the lease-end.

Lease for two or three years if you just want the fun of driving a particular fancy vehicle, and only if you are financially well off. If you must lease to have a manageable payment, then you can't afford what you're trying to get! Period! Leases always cost more in total!

I cannot even begin to count the number of customers that I see who are trying to trade out of long term leases. Getting caught up in the excitement of the moment, they take a five year lease on a cutesy little car and end up hating it in a few months. Then they come in trying to get out of it.

Maybe the thing you should do is to go to a car rental company and rent one of the models you think you may want. Drive it for a few days before you lock yourself into a contract. Above all, do not even consider leasing it for a long term.

Young people especially shouldn't look at leasing, because their needs and wants change more quickly than people who have owned dozens of vehicles, and whose employment and environment is more established.

When you're under a finance contract and hate your car, you'll have negative equity; when you're leasing and hate your car, you'll have negative equity plus lease penalties, if you try to get out.

To sum up, I know I've been very anti-leasing. I am speaking to you from 40+ years of experience. I've seen and done it all! Leasing may be fine for some people, but for 98% of all consumers, I say, do not even consider listening to a lease pitch! For the two percent that maybe should lease, be very careful and never, never, lease for over three years.

How A Lease Is Calculated

Let's take a look at a typical lease calculation. You can calculate your own lease with just a few known items.

Let's look at a three year lease with a vehicle that will lose 50% of its' MSRP value over 36 months (a dealer will give you this information if you ask). Set up your worksheet this way:

Say you qualify for a six percent interest rate.

MSRP	=	$34,000.00
Residual Value	=	$17,000.00
Depreciation	=	$17,000.00
Interest Rate	=	6%
Money Factor; 6.0 ÷ 2400 =		.0025

Capitalized Cost (selling price)	=	$34,000.00
Cap. Cost Reduction (down payment)	=	$0.00
Adjusted Cap. Cost	=	$34,000.00
Residual (.50 x 34000)	=	$17,000.00

Depreciation $= \$17,000.00$
Monthly Depreciation (17000 ÷ 36) $= \$472.22$

Calculating

Monthly rent charge

Adjusted Cap. Cost $= \$34,000.00$
Residual $+ \$17,000.00$
Total $= \$51,000.00$
Money Factor $= .0025$
(.0025 x $51,000.00)

$= \$127.50$

(This is your payment on the amount of money being financed.)

Calculating

Base and Total Payment

Monthly Depreciation $\$472.22$
Monthly Rental Charge $+ \$127.50$
Base Monthly Payment $= \$599.72$

So, you see it is not something that you can't do without the dealer. A bank or credit union can give you book values and can help you figure depreciation as a percentage of the Original MSRP.

Once you have that, multiply the percentage times the MSRP on the vehicle you're interested in leasing. (The other alternative is to just ask the dealer what the *residual percentage* and the *money factor* are.) They won't hide it from you if they're honest.

Anyway, once we have those two it's simple. Residual percentage times MSRP equals the end value. Subtract that from the *selling price*, the balance is the depreciation.

Divide your interest rate (APR) by 2400, which gives you the money factor. Residual times the money factor is your monthly rent.

Add the monthly depreciation to the monthly rent, and you have your payment, at the dealers' full price. But we don't want that do we?

So, looking at this example, let's negotiate! On a lease! Let's say we dicker back and forth, and finally the dealer agrees to sell you the car for $31,000.00 which means you have negotiated a savings of $3,000.00.

Remember that unless you express all of your knowledge about how to calculate a lease, the dealership still thinks they have an opportunity to make a large back end. It is not necessary to admit that you know how to calculate a lease in order to negotiate the capitalized cost. The dealer will try to convince you that, "Leases are unlike purchases, and they are not negotiable since you are not buying the vehicle." Don't buy the story, just insist on negotiating the price, and they will!

Look now at the dealers' proposal after agreeing to discount the capitalized cost (selling price) to $31,000.00.

Our residual stays the same, because it is a percentage of MSRP, but the dealer will try to make up the profit difference on the back end.

MSRP $34,000.00
Capitalized Cost $31,000.00
  (Your new selling price.)
Residual Value $17,000.00 (50% of MSRP)
Depreciation $14,000.00 ($31,000.00 - $17,000.00)
  ($3,000.00 less than it was.)
Money Factor .00416 (Notice what the dealer does. Remember, at this point, they don't know that you are able to calculate your own lease payments.)

Monthly Depreciation $388.89 ($14,000.00 ÷ 36)

Calculate monthly rent: (Dealer's figures)

Adjusted Cap Cost $31,000.00
Residual + $17,000.00
Total = $48,000.00
Money Factor .00416 x $199.68

And,

      Monthly Depreciation $388.89
        ($14{,}000 \div 36$ mo)

      Monthly Rental Charge $199.68

      New Payment $588.57

The new monthly depreciation is $83.33 per month lower; however, it looks like our $3,000.00 discount amounts to a little over $10.00 per month doesn't it? That's what the dealer hopes you will fall for.

See why a dealer will discount more easily for a non-educated lessee? He knows he likely can make it back up in the interest (back-end profit).

Now what do you suppose it would look like with no discount and still at the money factor of .00416? Remember, .00416 means an interest rate of 10%! ($.00416 \times 2400 = 9.984\%$ APR)

Now, how should your actual numbers look using the $31,000.00 price and the 6% APR you know you are able to qualify for?

      Calculate monthly rent: (your figures)

      Adjusted capital cost $31,000.00
          Residual   + $17,000.00
         Total   = $48,000.00
         Money factor .0025 (6%) x $48,000.00 = $120.00

Monthly depreciation; $31,000.00 minus residual of $17,000.00 = $14,000.00. $14,000.00 $\div$ 36 months = $388.89.

$120.00   monthly money charge
$388.89 +   monthly depreciation
$508.89   your payment

The dealer would have you believe the payment is $588.57. You see, by calculating your own lease payment, you save over $80.00 per month. The $80.00 per month you save amounts to just under

$3,000.00 in just three years. If a customer leases for five years, that's almost $5,000.00 over the period of the lease, and that money is extra profit over and above what the dealer makes on the vehicle itself. Negotiating keeps the money in your pocket, and from the original payment of $599.72 down to $508.89. That's $90.83 per month, and a total of $3,269.88 on your three year lease!

You see why I believe the average person needs to avoid getting involved in a lease, however; if you do lease, negotiate your capitalized cost (selling price) up front. Do not believe them if they tell you a lease can't be negotiated!

Now here are some more things to watch out for if you should still be interested in a lease.

Once you have negotiated a good deal on a lease, watch out! As you now will be introduced to the finance manager, who will prepare your paperwork. This party may be introduced as a business manager, or in some dealerships you won't actually meet anyone, as the paperwork is just sent back out with your salesperson, although this is highly unlikely, because they want another shot at you for more profit; some stores send the salesperson back out for the back-end profit.

Be careful now, because here's the place they try to sell you all the extra profit making items; paint and fabric sealants, life and disability insurance, alarm systems, GPS tracking devices, such as LoJack and HiJack, window tint, GAP insurance, and so many systems I can't begin to list them here.

They will tell you these things are to protect and enhance your value. You don't care! You're leasing the vehicle! Anything you buy extra is foolish! It's not your value that you will enhance if you buy something extra!

You don't add extras unless you're buying. Do not buy anything additional for a leased vehicle. You will be throwing your money away!

A lot of the GPS companies like LoJack may be fine in some places, but sometimes they only work within a small area close to where you bought it. The GPS areas are sometimes extremely limited in the geographic areas, and some as few as a ten mile radius!

They will tell you that the paint sealants will protect your residual value. They won't. The lease company expects to get the vehicle back with normal wear and tear. That includes rock chips. Anything that isn't normal will be too big and covered by your insurance anyway, such as dented fenders.

The only thing about adding things to a lease would be some original equipment difference that could be residualized. That would be like upgrading to the model with the factory moon roof that would be a part of the MSRP and would therefore be part of a higher residual value whereby you are not paying for the whole thing. If the vehicle has a 50% residual value, then switching to one with $1,000.00 more in factory equipment will mean you end up paying depreciation on $500.00 more over the lease.

Check your driving habits, and if you think you will drive less than you have been before, don't kid yourself, most people end up driving more. New vehicle, more fun, excitement, faster, showier, and you'll spend more time driving it. Guaranteed! A lot more!

If you really think you'll drive 20,000 miles per year, then have the lease calculated for that. The most wasteful thing you can do is limit your driving to hold down the miles, so give yourself enough! The other option, of course, is to just enjoy it, and pay the mileage penalty at the end. This will naturally be the most expensive way to do it. If you come down to where you have to carefully calculate mileage like this, I think you're nuts! Don't lease!

If you were on a purchase contract rather than a lease, the excess miles would still cost you money by lowering the value of your vehicle. So, one way or another, you will pay for the mileage you put on! Keep in mind however; the decreased amount of value is miniscule for higher miles on a financed vehicle! Also remember, that just because you leased the vehicle, you still have to keep up the maintenance, and the lessor may even have stricter maintenance intervals, but not too likely.

I see a gradual change happening in our automobile industry. The economy has people driving their vehicles longer, and a lot of these people are finding that it really makes sense to do so.

I'll repeat once more; never lease a vehicle with the intention of buying it at the end of the lease! If you really think you need to make sure you like it before you commit to buy, you're a lot better off to just finance it for a longer time, and if you don't like it, sell or trade it when you're ready. That gives you the control over the process from the very beginning. Plus that, if you finance originally at a new car rate, you just pay 'til it's done. If you leased and bought it out at the end, you'd pay a higher finance rate on the used car!

Buying your leased vehicle is like paying for it 1 ½ times, if you look at your lease costs, and add the purchase costs.

Yes, it costs more to lease vehicles than it does to purchase! Period.

LEE

CHAPTER 10
DON'T TRADE A PIG! CLEAN UP YOUR CAR

Whether you decide to trade in your present vehicle or to sell it on the market, there are some preparations you should take. The first rule of the car business is, what we in the business call *eyeball*. This means exactly what it implies: How a vehicle looks! If it looks good, or has good eyeball, it will sell well. Conversely, if the car looks like a dog, it will not sell well.

A good example of this is your own vehicle search. Do you look twice at vehicles that are ugly? Of course not! Car people are no different from anyone else. We look at your trade-in and form an instant impression of how well you cared for it. If your car is dirty, scratched, and smells bad, it will dramatically affect the value in our eyes. As a used car manager, I wouldn't even drive a pig!

My advice to you is to spend some time and or money on your trade before you bring it in. You may be a total slob in your everyday life, but you'd better step back and take a look at your car before you consider trading. I'm very serious about this, when I say to spend some time and or money, or both!

Most people in our society today live hectic lifestyles. The automobile is a necessity to get to work, shop, pick up the kids and becomes a means to an end. When you're using the car, truck, R.V. or minivan to shuttle kids, carpool and the like, it's amazing what gets lost between and under seats, ground into carpets, and hidden in all the nooks and crannies. Last year's french fries, gum, soda, pet hair and so forth. You may have an immaculate home and be so finicky about your personal appearance, but don't forget about your vehicle. It can cost you a lot of money. More than you could imagine! I can tell you that a super-clean car can bring an average of one to two thousand dollars more than a dirty rat! We appraisers always feel we can see through dirt, but we can all be swayed by a very clean vehicle because if it's clean on the inside and outside, chances are that is has also been well-maintained. If it's filthy, I will assume that you also do not maintain it well! This is common sense, and oh so important to you; unless you don't need one or two thousand extra dollars!

Now let's talk about your preparation. I recommend having your trade-in professionally detailed before you even consider trying to trade it in. If you decide to sell your car yourself and not pay to have it professionally detailed, here are some tips to help you:

> Check your oil, if it's dirty, change both oil and filter. If the oil is clean, make sure to add some if needed.

> Fill the windshield washer reservoir (shows good care). Even if it's inoperative, if it's full, I won't test it.

> Scrub the engine and engine compartment. There are all sorts of automotive degreasers and cleaners for this. If you don't care to go to the extra expense, use a common household cleanser. Scrub as best you can and rinse with hot water to loosen caked grease and grime. Then wipe down every part where water will leave spots, such as the air cleaner cover, fan shroud, etc.

> If you have any rusted places under the hood, spray these areas with gloss black lacquer paint. This will give it a like new appearance to the valve covers, etc.

> Spray spark plug wires, hoses and other parts with a clear gloss lacquer (after they are clean — of course). Hold a stiff piece of cardboard behind anything you are painting to avoid overspray.

Make sure to clean the underside of the hood also.

Now let's go to the trunk. If the mat is stained, take it out and scrub it with soap and a stiff brush. Rinse, and hang up to dry. It will come out surprisingly nice!

Check the spare tire. If it's dirty or used, take it and scrub it with cleanser. Then when it's dry, spray it with clear lacquer. Yes, the rubber also. You can also paint the tread with black paint to give it the illusion of more tread depth if it's been used (use a brush and paint only the tread). The pros do it!

If you are a smoker, take out the ashtray and scrub it. Also scrub the headliner, carpet and seats. Make sure you're doing this cleaning at a time when you can allow the car to dry properly, as nothing smells worse than wet carpet. Also, the cleaning will heighten the smell of stale smoke, so you need for it to dry. Then, you'd better avoid smoking in it until it sells.

Take a small brush, such as a toothbrush and cotton swabs, and clean the air vents, knobs and hard to get at crevices on the dash. Follow with a silicone based product on the dash, foot pedals, and leather or vinyl seats. Armor All® works well. I knew the inventor. He was a close friend of John Wayne.

Remove all window stickers, bumper stickers, and personal signs from the vehicle. Nobody cares if you've been to Yellowstone. Especially get your political signs off the car, and off the bumpers!

After the inside is thoroughly clean, start on the outside. Rust on chrome bumpers and wheel covers is easily removed with fine steel wool and cleanser. Also remove any rust from the antenna.

Dingy looking body-side moldings can be brought to life with fine steel wool and silicone. If not, they're cheap to replace. Get it done beforehand, because even though the dealer can do it cheaper, you need that good first impression!

If you have one of those occasional scratches that get in your windshield when a wiper blade goes bad before you can turn it off, there is a solution; toothpaste and a damp cloth. You read it right, toothpaste! It will take a lot of scrubbing, but it will take the scratches out and make a world of difference. There are of course, products you can buy to also do these things.

If you have a star in your windshield, your insurance will probably cover to have it fixed at no charge to you, and no effect on your rates. They'd rather do that than take a chance on buying a whole windshield later on, so have it done. Otherwise, a dealer deducts at least $200.00 from the appraisal; figuring to either repair or replace it. He figures this, because if a repair fails, he will need to be covered.

Scrub your wheels and tires. Cleanser and a stiff brush works well on raised white letters. When they're dry, wipe them dry and spray them with silicone.

If you have chipped or marred steel wheels, paint them. You can do it right on the car by masking around the tire with tape, newspaper and cardboard.

Now go back over the car. Did you remember the door jambs and inside the fuel door?

If you have rock chips or small scratches that you have decided not to pay to have airbrushed, there is a sneaky way to effectively make them less visible. I have done this before, and while not perfect, it's better than doing nothing. Take a selection of colored pencils, find the color closest to a match, wet the tip and rub it into the scratch. It may take a combination of colors, but keep applying until the scratch or chip fades.

Now apply a good paste wax, taking care to first let the touchup dry thoroughly. Wipe it off with a terry towel and even your scratches will now be a lot less noticeable, if not invisible from ten feet away. I've even used magic markers and ball point pens before waxing it.

When you are about to show the car to a prospect and you really have a lot of apparent scratches or swirls from carwashes, do what a dealer would do. Rinse the car with water just before they arrive and leave it wet. The water will mask a myriad of flaws, and the only thing your prospective buyer thinks is, "How nice, they washed it for me."

Otherwise, spend a hundred dollars or so to get it detailed right. If you have a cracked windshield, get it replaced! It's cheaper for you to do under your insurance than what a dealer will deduct from the value. Remember that first impressions count for or against you. If you are running around with a broken windshield, a used car manager will wonder what else you have ignored. Maybe, even though the manager may not detect any engine or transmission problems, he will not only look harder for problems, but likely any glaring problems will cost you extra, because it just makes an appraiser figure there will be much more wrong!

I always appraised vehicles that had things obviously wrong, with the idea that maintenance had probably not been performed properly, and I'd give it a lower value to allow for hidden problems. If you have rock chips or scratches on your vehicle, use one of the airbrushing companies I describe in the chapter on buying a used vehicle. Even though a dealer can have this service done for less money than it will cost you. Again; the first impression your vehicle makes is most important. If your tires are bad, buy a cheap new set. If the dealer looks at your tires as being in need of replacement, he may deduct from four to eight hundred dollars from your car's value. If your vehicle needs wheel covers or center caps, try to get this done before trying to trade. Sure, the dealer can do some of these things, and you can argue the fact that he can buy cheaper than you can.

Remember this though, even if the dealer's parts and service departments can buy cheaper than you can, they charge the dealer's sales department full retail price. Therefore, since it is the sales department with whom you must deal, get it done beforehand. You may buy from a discount store, while the dealer's parts department charges much more, but the used car manager must buy in-house.

You also must keep uppermost in your mind that the condition of your trade-in forms an opinion as to how we judge that you have maintained the rest of your car. If we see a car with bad tires, for example, we will assume that if you haven't the money to run safe tires for your family, then you probably haven't changed oil or performed normal maintenance on the rest of the vehicle. I always trained my sales staff to not judge the customer by what they drive. The one exception is the family vehicle with bad tires. Anyone who travels with their family on bad tires probably cannot afford much, or they wouldn't take such a chance with their loved ones. When we suspect that you haven't kept up your maintenance, we will give you a whole lot less money for your trade!

When we appraise a trade-in, we first walk around it to form an overall impression of not only what we will estimate for reconditioning, but also in many cases, how thorough an appraisal we must do. If your trade-in looks well taken care of, and it shows pride of ownership, then maybe no one will even take it for a drive! Especially when we're having a busy day. On the other hand, if we judge that the car is rough, meaning it will need a lot of expense for reconditioning, then we will more carefully check the engine, transmission, etc. I can't even count the times over the years when the only thing that killed the value on the customer's trade was because it was filthy! Sometimes I wouldn't even sit down in the car because I didn't want to soil my clothes; I just killed the appraisal value! Like I mentioned previously, and I will repeat it; if you don't realize how much of a slob you are, let a professional detailer do the job. Not to hurt anybody's feelings, but some of us don't realize how unkempt we are, and an outside opinion may make you money! A Realtor® won't sell your house until you clean it up, and there is no sense losing money on your dirty car!

The appraiser must make a guess as to how costly the cleanup will be.

Some vehicles come in so dirty, that it's questionable as to whether or not we can clean an interior or if we might have to replace it. I've seen values decrease more than three thousand dollars for such things as stained seats, filthy carpets, smells such as spilled milk and other causes. In most instances, these vehicles have finally cleaned up okay, but it's that first impression that we make when we do an appraisal that counts. Spend the money up front, give yourself the advantage! Whatever you spend will be an investment that will come back to you five to ten times over and maybe a lot more. Don't be cheap when you're trading or selling your vehicle. Does it look like a dealer's used car? No; then handle it!

What about the customer with the slipping transmission? Wouldn't you rather we didn't drive it? Sure, you can say, "I wouldn't lie," but 95% of all buyers wouldn't hesitate not mentioning it. This is a reverse Caveat Emptor, where the dealer being the buyer must beware! It boils down to the fact that if we don't catch it, we eat it! Now you can see why we always teach our salespeople; buyers are liars.

You may be one of those honest buyers out there who would actually tell up us front, but believe me when I say you are in the minority! Once we take your trade-in, anything we find wrong with it, we're stuck with it. We can't call you back and say, "You cheated us!" It just doesn't work in reverse!

We don't even hate the customer for it because we're used to it. The public in general sees nothing wrong with cheating a car dealer. That is an accepted fact that we deal with. If you state to us that you don't know of anything wrong with your car, and we miss it, we're stuck. So, as I said before, if you don't want us to find everything wrong with your trade, then make it look as good cosmetically as you can before you bring it in, and hope we don't drive it.

I remember back a few years when a customer had almost finished all of his paperwork when the manager (who seldom drove any trade-ins during the appraisal) decided he'd better drive the trade. It was very dirty so he figured he'd better see how it ran. When it wouldn't start, he opened the hood and guess what? No engine! None at all! The customer had towed the vehicle close to the dealership and then got in it and coasted down the hill, right in to the parking area directly in front of the showroom.

This customer knew through friends about the manager's lack of careful appraising and almost got away with it. Had it been clean, he would have. In this particular instance, the manager told me he only went to drive it because it was so filthy he got worried.

On busy days, there are a great many managers who appraise vehicles in this same manner. They walk around it, look at the overall condition, and make quick decisions. Use these sloppy methods to your advantage.

One mega-dealer I worked for had the sales office upstairs. All decisions were made from this office, and driving appraisals were almost never done. Volume was so heavy that they might sell forty or fifty cars in a day, which meant maybe seventy appraisals, counting sales that they didn't make! That's just too much business to have time for careful appraisals. Sure, they got a bad engine or transmission now and then, but for a huge volume dealer, that was just part of doing business. In that case, eyeball was the key factor!

Keep in mind that when you are trading in a vehicle, you are the salesman for your own product. Make sure it represents you well!

This chapter is also extremely important when you advertise your car for sale online, or in paper publications.

CHAPTER 11
BECOME YOUR OWN SALESPERSON

Some people will try to sell their own vehicle through the newspaper or one of the private magazines and car shopper services available. The same rules of preparation apply, only with a twist!

Not only should you prepare the vehicle you're selling but also you must now prepare your showroom. That's right, your showroom! By this, I mean your front yard. Clean up the kids' toys, mow your lawn, and otherwise clean your place up to reflect a pride of ownership in your home as well as the car. Face it, the overall impression you give of yourself, your home, and your car can and will affect your value. Let me give you an example of what I mean. Who would you rather buy a used vehicle from; someone who owns a neat looking home and appears at the door in clean clothes, or a guy in a filthy t-shirt and two days growth of beard, and the lawn is overgrown, and the house is a pig sty? He meets you at the door with a cigarette dangling from his mouth and a beer in his hand. Well?

It's a lot like going out to look at used car lots. If you drive on to a lot that looks really dirty and the office windows are dirty, the floors filthy and trash all around the place, you can easily be dissuaded from even looking at any cars. A customer will correctly assume that if a dealer doesn't keep up his lot, he may also not keep up the condition of his inventory, no matter how it appears. On the other hand, a dealer with a clean and well cared for facility is easier to believe will have better vehicles. Even an old shack of a building works if it's painted and clean.

Remember this, when someone comes over to look at the car you are selling, make sure your inventory, your dealership (home) and salesperson (you) are well prepared to receive buyers. First impressions count for a lot, and you don't get a chance to start over. You are your own salesman now, so look in the mirror!

Now as far as pricing goes, be careful. There are so many vehicles on the market, that being far out of line price-wise is a waste of money. If there are twenty vehicles in the paper similar to yours, you'd better be competitive or your phone won't ring. A lot of consumers like buying direct from the seller so they can meet the owner, see what you look like, and ask questions about your experience with the vehicle. People feel the private seller is more trustworthy than the average car salesperson, but keep in mind, that you still must make that good impression. Also, you are now competing with the car dealer who can take trade-ins and offer financing to his buyers. Make sure your price is well within line.

A lot of people try to sell their vehicle themselves because they aren't satisfied with the trade allowance offered by dealers. A great many people are tricked into doing this by the car dealer!

If you owe a balance on the vehicle you are trying to replace, under no circumstances should you ever buy the new one with the idea that you will sell your other one later on! Unless you are in a comfortable financial position; absolutely never, ever consider doing this! I cannot emphasize this strongly enough! It will trap you! About 80% of the time! Now here, I'm not talking about a free and clear vehicle with a low value, but if you have a car with a balance owing, and try this, you can get in bad trouble!

People every day get caught up in the excitement of the new car deal and agree to do stupid things. Take the situation of the purchaser who for whatever reason, believes that his vehicle is worth so much more than the dealer is giving him that he will succumb to the dealer's suggestion that he, "Buy the new one now and sell his trade himself."

The dealer convinces this customer that he should have no problem getting what he feels his car is worth but because of the sale price of the new car he can't give him that much. The dealer offers to delay the first payment for a month and a half to three months or so to allow the customer adequate time to sell his vehicle before the payments on the new one begin. Now, this knowledgeable buyer has a limited time to dispose of his first vehicle, and if he cannot do so, he will be faced with two payments, one of which he can't afford. Don't even consider this unless you can easily handle both payments, and then your sale can drag out.

Even though the dealer has thoroughly convinced you that you'll never get an opportunity like this again, walk away from it. There's always another chance of a lifetime. Always! Anytime you find a car deal that's too good to be true, if it involves this sort of compromise to own it, walk or run away!

If you feel that you cannot justify the trade allowance being offered by the dealer and are convinced that you will benefit substantially by selling your trade yourself, then do so. Then, buy the other vehicle after you have sold your vehicle first. People often worry that if they take the time to sell their vehicle by themselves, then when it sells, they won't have a car. Big deal! So you rent a car for a while until you get out and buy a new one. Even if the dealer may not have the vehicle in stock that you want, it is quite likely that he will give you a loaner vehicle until yours gets in, once a deal is made. Make certain to negotiate that in your deal.

Buying the new one now and trying the private party sale afterwards, accounts for a huge percentage of repossessions and ruination of credit for years afterward. A good example of how this works to the dealer's benefit is the case of the trade-in that has an actual cash value far below wholesale book. Take a vehicle with a low book figure of $24,000.00 that no dealer would own for more than $19,000.00, due to current market conditions that only the dealer knows. It's really easy to show the customer that if he sells it himself with a wholesale value of $24,000.00 and a retail book value of $29,000.00 he should have no problem selling it himself for at least $24,000.00 because that's wholesale. Here's where a buyer can be so easily misled. Most people think that whatever the book says is the gospel. That the books don't lie, and dealers go by them 100 percent! The dealer will now capitalize on this, and easily convince this hapless soul to kick the trade (remove it from the deal)! What this customer doesn't realize is that any dealer who owns one like his, could sell it for $20,000.00 and still make a profit of $1,000.00 since he would own it for no more than $19,000.00. Now this customer is in for a huge and costly experience when he tries to sell it. One needs to understand that the dealer does this for a living, and if he can't find a buyer for your car, what chance do you have? He's the expert! Do you really think you are a better car salesman than the dealer?

This is precisely the reason that we look at book value only as a guide and must know what the ACV (actual cash value) is, and its' relationship to the book. The way to do this correctly is ascertain what price you can purchase the vehicle you want for. Then, advertise your vehicle. When you have the *cash in fist* (CIF) go back to the dealer and buy your new one. Oh, don't worry; if a price is good now, it can and will be available at the same price later! Seldom can any price not be duplicated later on.

Another facet to this same problem is the case where the customer's desire for the new vehicle is so overwhelming that they heed the salesperson's dishonest advice to, "Buy this one now and give the other one back to the lender." Great! A voluntary repossession is still a repossession! It will stay on your credit records and ruin your credit for at least ten years into the future. That's stupid! Don't do it! Never, ever!

The way this is often done, is the unscrupulous salesperson convinces the customer that the reason they are so buried in their trade is because their last dealer cheated them! He then goes on to tell them if they let it go back, it won't hurt their credit because the other dealer has to buy it back from their bank, telling them he has a repurchase agreement. Recourse agreements used to be a big part of the car business, and some still are; but before a dealer is forced to buy back your vehicle from the bank, you must first let the bank repossess it! Result = credit ruined! Then, even if the dealer had a backup guarantee on your loan, the repossession still stays as a permanent record on your credit.

This next method is called *butter-nosing* the trade. Sometimes the dealer will push very hard to get you to leave the trade out of the equation by saying things such as, "It can't hurt your credit anymore," or "Your credit score really can't go any lower, and by the time the repossession is reported, your new loan on this car will already be on the report, cancelling out the repo." "Then make your payments on time on your new car, and your credit will soon be reestablished." This is really a rotten thing to do to people, but it goes on all the time!

Well, it won't cancel out! What about the other lender selling that repossessed vehicle, and of course, for a loss! Yes, of course they will lose money because; otherwise the dealer would have been able to take it in trade if it were worth what you owe.

When the lender sells this vehicle and loses money, he will now come after you for the deficiency balance. Anytime you allow a vehicle to go back to a lender, it is a repossession, and it makes not one bit of difference on a credit report if it is voluntary, or involuntary, and whether or not the lender loses money, or how much. It still counts the same. Even if the lender managed to sell the vehicle for a profit, you still have a repo!

When you have a repossession, you will be liable for any loss the resulting re-sale will realize. The lender will also be able to charge you for all the costs of repossession and sale, including legal fees, mileage, storage, auction fees, and a lot more! They may garnish your paychecks, file liens on property and keep after you continually for the balance. They will stay on you. Many people end up getting behind in the payments on their newly purchased vehicle because of ruthless collecting on the repossessed one. Don't take the chance! Trade or don't buy! No vehicle is worth buying if it will cause you this kind of grief!

A repossession may also cost you your job! If you are in any security connected position, or most all jobs where you have higher responsibilities, this could hit you hard. More and more, companies require employees to have good credit records, as it reflects on their honesty and integrity.

I cannot stress too much how many people are slickered into

defaulting on a financial obligation by some silver-tongued thief! The public is so ignorant as to the legal consequences and the long term damage that can result from defaulting on a car loan, that in the excitement of buying the feel good, they ruin their futures!

Now that you know what you need to do to change your future vehicle buying habits, I want to sincerely wish you success!

When you have made your first great deal, please recommend this book to others.

Thank you,

Lee

APR		NUMBER OF MONTHS					
	24	30	36	48	60	72	84
4.00	0.04342	0.03508	0.02952	0.02258	0.01842	0.01564	0.01367
5.00	0.04387	0.03553	0.02997	0.02303	0.01887	0.01611	0.01413
5.50	0.04409	0.03575	0.03019	0.02325	0.01910	0.01634	0.01437
5.75	0.04421	0.03586	0.03031	0.02337	0.01922	0.01645	0.01449
6.00	0.04432	0.03598	0.03042	0.02349	0.01933	0.01657	0.01461
6.25	0.04443	0.03609	0.03054	0.02360	0.01945	0.01669	0.01473
6.50	0.04455	0.03620	0.03065	0.02371	0.01957	0.01681	0.01485
6.75	0.04466	0.03632	0.03076	0.02383	0.01968	0.01693	0.01497
7.00	0.04477	0.03643	0.03088	0.02395	0.01980	0.01705	0.01509
7.25	0.04488	0.03654	0.03099	0.02406	0.01992	0.01717	0.01522
7.50	0.04500	0.03666	0.03111	0.02418	0.02004	0.01729	0.01534
7.75	0.04511	0.03677	0.03122	0.02430	0.02020	0.01741	0.01546
8.00	0.04523	0.03689	0.03134	0.02441	0.02028	0.01753	0.01559
8.25	0.04534	0.03700	0.03145	0.02453	0.02040	0.01765	0.01571
8.50	0.04546	0.03712	0.03157	0.02465	0.02052	0.01778	0.01584
8.75	0.04560	0.03723	0.03170	0.02477	0.02064	0.01790	0.01596
9.00	0.04568	0.03735	0.03180	0.02489	0.02076	0.01803	0.01609
9.25	0.04580	0.03746	0.03192	0.02500	0.02088	0.01815	0.01622
9.50	0.04591	0.03758	0.03203	0.02512	0.02100	0.01827	0.01634
9.75	0.04603	0.03769	0.03215	0.02524	0.02112	0.01840	0.01647
10.00	0.04614	0.03781	0.03227	0.02536	0.02125	0.01853	0.01660
11.00	0.04661	0.03828	0.03274	0.02585	0.02174	0.01903	0.01712
12.00	0.04707	0.03875	0.03321	0.02633	0.02224	0.01955	0.01765
13.00	0.04754	0.03922	0.03369	0.02683	0.02275	0.02007	0.01819
14.00	0.04801	0.03970	0.03418	0.02733	0.02327	0.02061	0.01874
15.00	0.04849	0.04018	0.03467	0.02783	0.02379	0.02115	0.01930
18.00	0.04992	0.04164	0.03615	0.02937	0.02539	0.02281	0.02102
20.00	0.05090	0.04263	0.03716	0.03043	0.02649	0.02395	0.02221
22.00	0.05188	0.04363	0.03819	0.03151	0.02762	0.02513	0.02343
25.00	0.05337	0.04516	0.03976	0.03316	0.02935	0.02694	0.02531
30.00	0.05591	0.04778	0.04245	0.03601	0.03235	0.03008	0.02859

www.ingramcontent.com/pod-product-compliance
Lightning Source LLC
Chambersburg PA
CBHW060510290526
45791CB00001B/349